*Tim. Wishin...
Happy ;*

C000079450

Ayrshire Golf
& Chapter
Verse

by

Peter J Bond

*with love
George & Wendy
x*

Lang**Syne**
PUBLISHING
WRITING *to* REMEMBER

Lang Syne

PUBLISHING

WRITING *to* REMEMBER

79 Main Street, Newtongrange,
Midlothian EH22 4NA
Tel: 0131 344 0414   Fax: 0845 075 6085
E-mail: info@lang-syne.co.uk
www.langsyneshop.co.uk

Design by Dorothy Meikle
Photographs by Archie McKie
Printed by Printwell Ltd
© Peter J Bond 2016

ISBN 978-1-85217-679-2

Contents

I should like to dedicate this book to my parents:-
John M. Bond and Margaret M. Bond

Thanks to:-
John Millar, who offered encouragement,
optimism, direction, and whose contacts
helped get things off the ground.
His input was very helpful and
greatly appreciated.

Special Thanks to:-
My good friend Archie McKie, who has
a successful Building and Engineering Business
in Irvine, a keen golfer and member of
Ravenspark Golf Club, who came up with
the concept for this book, and without whose
foresight, encouragement, guidance,
optimism, belief, drive and determination,
this book would not have come to fruition.
I shall be eternally grateful for his contribution.

Tee-ing Off!

Poetry has become a relatively recent passion but golf has been my life since as a 14 year-old schoolboy I started playing at Ravenspark Golf Club in Irvine.

My game was self-taught from golf books and within four years I had turned professional.

I played on the European Tour and the Tartan Tour; playing Tournament golf throughout Britain and Europe alongside the likes of Sam Torrance, Seve Ballesteros, Ian Woosnam, Jack Newton, Brian Barnes and Sandy Lyle.

I had qualified as a PGA Professional from the PGA school at the same time as Sam Torrance and the examiner's report stated that I had...'the ability to do well in the profession'.

Obviously I never achieved the heights that Sam Torrance scaled, but in a modest way, I had my moments.

At Cathcart Castle in Glasgow, I broke the Professional Course Record with a 65, which stood for a number of years until Bernard Gallacher eventually bettered it.

In the British Under 25's Championship I was paired with the Irishman John O'Leary, who was a successful young European Tour player, featuring regularly on television.

We were both level playing the seventeenth where I took six and he made a birdie.

In the changing room afterwards O'Leary approached and said he had been impressed by my standard of play and but for one hole I could have had a solid round.

We struck up a friendship and any time we met at tournaments we would play together in practice rounds.

There were many encounters with other well-known figures from the world of golf. In 1973 at Kilmarnock Barassie I played with Sam Torrance and Peter Alliss in the pre-qualifying for the Open Championship at Royal Troon.

In 1974, in the British Match Play Championship at Downfield, Dundee, I was drawn against the Australian Jack Newton, who had already won European events, and would later lose a play-off against Tom Watson for the 1975 Open at Carnoustie.

John O'Leary invited me to join him for a practice round prior to the first round ties, and invited me to play a fourball with him, Christy O'Connor Jnr. and Eamon Darcy – both of whom were up and coming golfers and future Ryder Cup stars.

On the day of my tie with Jack Newton, I was understandably nervous at drawing the favourite to win the event, but I was one under par when the talented Aussie beat me 4/3. Newton then went on to win the final for another Tour victory that season.

That same year, I finished third in the four round Scottish Assistant's Championship after leading at the halfway mark.

After failing to qualify for the 1975 Open Championship at Carnoustie by a couple of shots, I was standing at the 18th tee spectating, when Jack Nicklaus, Tom Weiskopf, Jack Newton and John O'Leary, who were playing a practice round, approached the tee.

Jack Newton nodded, but John O'Leary beckoned me to come through the fence and walk up the eighteenth with them. We had a chat as we walked, but John would know that few people get to walk up the eighteenth with Jack Nicklaus, and that he was letting a friend share in that experience.

I returned to Downfield, Dundee, to win their Pro-am in 1977.

In 1979, I qualified – with two rounds in the 60s at the qualifier over Belleisle – for the European Open at Turnberry.

On visiting the practice ground before my first round I was surprised to find that the spectator stand was full, and then I saw why...Seve Ballesteros was practising.

The only space left on the practice ground was between Seve, and Ken Brown. There was nothing else for it but to take a big gulp and park myself between them, hoping that I didn't hit Seve's caddy with a wayward golf ball while he was fielding for him.

One of my rounds was a 75 with 38 putts, one of Sandy Lyle's was a 65 with 28 putts. That was the difference between success and failure, Sandy won and I missed the cut.

Although I had numerous successes in Pro-ams etc., I never managed to make the breakthrough required to make a living playing tournaments and retired from tournament golf in 1994, to concentrate on my Club Pro's job at Ravenspark Golf Club from where I started my journey.

Poetry evolved as a pastime, and with some guidance and encouragement from my good friend, Archie McKie, who came up with the idea to combine my professional course management skills, and experience of playing golf courses, with poetry, we decided on this book.

It's a poetic look at some of the finest courses in Ayrshire...land o' Burns and home of golf.

The book is a guide in how to manage your way around these great courses, and obviously I appreciate that different conditions may require some adjustments to the clubs that I suggest you choose, but the way to play them would be the same.

Peter Bond

Peter J Bond

Royal Troon G.C.

Founded in 1878, Open Championship venue Royal Troon welcome you to their Royal Toon

Your **opening** tee shot is with a three wood
down the right hand side is good
leaving only a wedge or nine
err long cos big is fine

A three wood at the **second** on the right hand trap's your line
mid to short iron is fine
erring strong cos there are no bunkers at the back
so you can safely attack

The **third** hole play an iron or fairway wood from the tee
short right of the burn is the place to be
leaving a shortish iron to the flag
and again no bunkers at the back

Drive down the left fading in at the **fourth** hole par five
now it's a big three wood to reach the green from a good drive
don't be concerned if you don't get up
you can make up for it with a pitch and a putt

Take a long iron at the par three **fifth** over the bunker on the right
don't worry if the ball doesn't bite
cos there's no trouble if you're long
so again attack strong

Unless downwind at the par five **sixth** play a three wood on the
    left trap with a fade
same shot again cos the green can't be made
now a wedge to the right side of the green
you can hole the putt for a birdie if you're keen
downwind go for a big drive drawing from the right
then a three wood from the right might make it just might

At the **seventh** take an iron or fairway wood
play short of the bunkers if you could
now a mid iron to the back half
a par won't be the worst score to have

Now the famous Postage Stamp **eighth** hole par three
at 123 yards why is it world famous but you see
with such a narrow green surrounded by sand
set on a plateau but much lower than the tee you understand
the degree of difficulty being the height of the tee
and the prevailing wind from the sea
without the wind it's just a wedge to the target
and no problem landing on the carpet
but into a wind for such a short shot to be keeping the ball low
you have to play too strong a club for its length and so
you're punching a seven or eight iron into a wedge length
and the difficulty is in its strength
the ideal shot is to land middle left of the flag
giving you a chance of a birdie to bag
but if you allow the ball to drift slightly right
it will need to have plenty of bite
to prevent it kicking off the green into deep sand
or to give you more pressure than you can stand
running down the slope into a fifteen foot hollow
which can only end in grief and sorrow
but in trying to avoid all that if you were to miss the green to the left
you would be absolutely bereft
if your next shot shot across the green and down the slope
and if you left your third shot short you could lose all hope
of ever getting on the green at all
and may even pick up your ball
which is how the famous Postage Stamp leaves its mark
and why golfers play here from dawn till dark

A three wood off the tee at **nine**
on the left traps with a fade is fine
leaving a mid iron to the green
err short if you dont want the out of bounds seen

Play a three wood again at **ten**
middle right of fairway then
a mid to long iron up the left side
and hopefully a tough par can't hide

The railway hole number **eleven**
could have been designed in heaven
and from the championship tee
nothing less than a driver it will be
just to clear the gorse
but not too far of course
or you'll run out of fairway on the far side
so from this tee shot you cannot hide
you must take it on down the left with a fade
running with the fairway when all's been said
putting you in a position that could
reach the green with a long iron or wood
play it on the left trap with a fade
hitting this green would be well played

Driver at **twelve** down the left fading in
leaves a longish iron to the pin
over the left trap to the upper tier
take enough club and have no fear
this is the hole with Arnold Palmer's plaque
in the left semi rough from where he launched his attack
to put his ball on the green
one of the best shots ever seen

so they put the plaque there to commemorate
and everyone can see the shot he faced and the date

Hit your drive down the left at **thirteen**
now a long iron or wood if you're keen
to reach this green and more
to help protect your score

At the **fourteenth** hole par three
take plenty of club and see
if you can carry the trouble and land
on the green and not in the sand

On the left hand trap with a fade for your drive at **fifteen**
now for the green to be seen
needs a long iron or fairway wood
on the left trap with a fade could be good

Unless downwind at **sixteen** play short of the ditch
and to leave yourself with just a pitch
play a fairway wood over the left hand sand
now you'll putt for a birdie if everything goes as planned

Seventeenth par three
your tee shot will need to be
a long iron or fairway wood
faded in from the left if you could

Three wood from the **eighteenth** tee
right of centre is the place to be
then a longish iron fading in from the left traps
and the final green should be made perhaps

So there you have reached the end of your 'roon'
round Open Championship venue Royal Troon.

Old Prestwick G.C.

Prestwick Golf Club, founded 1851,
is a famous seaside links on the
Ayrshire coast
where Willie Park, in 1860, won the
first Open Championship of course
Old Tom Morris was Keeper of the
Green
his original layout can still be seen

This **opening** hole can bite
with the railway all the way down the right
on both your first shot and your second
the railway line can beckon
so take an iron on the tee
and aim down the left as it will bend you'll see
the railway attracts the ball like a magnet
collecting balls like a fisherman's dragnet
hit the fairway here
you'll deserve a beer
but you want to be far enough to catch the downslope
then you'll only have a nine or a wedge with which to cope
your second shot should err strong
as there's no real trouble long
but to the right lies the railway wall
and short left has a bunker to catch your ball

Second hole par three is surrounded by sand except back right
so if you find the bunkers make the green a bit tight
although middle of the green is where you'd prefer
a mid iron to the back right is where you should err

Par five **third** is one of the best holes you'll see
you have to think all the way to the green from the tee
an iron or fairway wood to start
as the fairway you must part
and lay up as close to the middle bunker as you dare
the closer you are the better you'll fare
now with a fairway wood you can go for the green
once over the Cardinal there are no more bunkers to be seen
attack from the left and hope for a good kick
if you don't make the green the right pitch you can pick

From the **fourth** tee launch a drive over the left hand bunker with
    a fade
don't worry about the semi-rough cos the twelfth fairway can be
    made
keeping well away from the Pow burn
running up the right side at every turn
you are now only left with an eight or nine
bunker short left so big is fine

The par three **fifth** is blind and tough
from the tee to the top of the hill lies deep rough
once over the hill all the trouble is left, and short right
so overclub and aiming right is bright
if you do miss back right of the green
the back to front slope will be clearly seen
and remember when you are pitching back on
that leaving a downhill putt will be frowned upon
so looking back at the green from the next tee
you can reminisce on a truly wonderful par three

Hit down the left of the **sixth** with a three wood
the idea being to hit a full second shot that'll stop good
the right half of the green is protected by a slope
and to bump and run would be hit and hope

On the **seventh** tee drive over the left bunker fading in
then a well struck long iron up the hill fading towards the pin
on a green sloping back to front and left to right
leaving your ball below the cup will delight

Down the right side with your drive at the **eighth** hole drawing
    round
then a longish iron to the back left of the pin needs found
better than in sand is the short cut
even if it leaves a downhill putt

Ninth tee is a superb driving hole down the right side
your second shot has nowhere to hide
aim a long iron on the left greenside bunker landing short
the slope on the fairway and green will leave you an uphill shot
a putt or a chip, whatever you favour
can make you a four and a par to savour

Hit your drive at the **tenth** on the left hand trap fading right
now a long iron or fairway wood on the left edge just might
kick down to the middle of the green
for a solid par four to be seen

At the par three **eleventh** take a long iron favouring back right
with the slope and wind from the sea big will be alright
but be careful putting back to the flag
downhill and downwind makes your putt difficult to lag

Go for a big drive at the par five **twelfth** down the right hand side
then a three wood from the right drifting in with the tide
if you don't reach all that's required is a good pitch
you can still get a birdie if it goes without a hitch

Another big drive down the right at **thirteen**
then a long iron coming in from the right sets the scene
with the humps and bumps throwing the ball away from the target
there's no guarantee of getting on to the carpet
but if you can get down in two and make four
you can indeed be proud of that score

A three wood at **fourteen** down the left with a fade
then deciding between an eight or nine is a trade
long and left is safe but long and right is out of bounds
so perhaps a big nine is sound

Five wood at **fifteen** from the tee
over the left bunker you see
again it's between an eight or a nine
with the slope of the green nine's fine
if landed on the left side
where the slope will take the ball for a ride
and transport it to the bottom right of the green
where just about everyone else has been

Drive at the **sixteenth** over Willie Campbell's grave
cos good fortune favours the brave
keep up the left and all will be bound
to kick towards the green because of the ground
leaving a good chance of a three
trust me you'll see

Seventeenth's a fairway wood at the start
cos you've a narrow fairway to part
you now have a blind second shot over the Alps
be careful this hole has collected many scalps
from the top of the Alps to the green lies a hidden fifty yards
fifty yards which have ruined many cards
cos here lies the Sahara bunker covering the whole width of the
    green
with steps down to the sand where many have been
go in here and you have no easy escape route
might even be fried egged to boot
after a few attempts you may even think it's fine
if you can walk away with only a nine
so you need a good mid iron landing at the back coming down
    off the slope
leaving you a putt to hole you hope

A driver aimed at the clock's your target
kicking the ball onto the carpet
leaving the **eighteenth** at the mercy of your skill
and a putt for an eagle or birdie still

So there is the course Old Tom first started
before heading back to St. Andrews he parted
What would Willie Park score here now
I'm sure he'd get it round somehow.

Trump Turnberry Ailsa

*Trump Turnberry is an
   Open Championship venue
   on the Ayrshire coast
   where you can enjoy a unique
   experience with Donald Trump
   as your host*

Your **opening** tee shot is an iron or fairway wood
aimed at the left bunker with a fade will be good
leaving a mid iron coming in from the right hand line
bunkers are all at the front so slightly big is fine

Inside the left trap with a fade for your drive at the **second** hole
 par four
then a mid to long iron between the traps to make your hopes
 soar
so long as you err towards the back
you'll keep your score on track

Hit driver at the **third** drawing in from the right
as the bunkers on the left make that approach tight
then a long iron or fairway wood fading from the left side
avoids the traps to the right where your ball can hide

Longish iron at the **fourth** drawing from the right hand side
keeps you away from the beach at low and high tide
you'll have done well between you and me
if you can escape from this hole with a par three

At the **fifth** a driver short of the right trap is the shot
then a wood drawing from the right and this green can be caught
if you miss short right you can still make four
with a pitch and putt to steady your score

Sixth hole par three needs a mid iron on the left trap with a fade
hit this green and two putt and a really good par has been made
missing the green to the right the ground falls away by far
leaving a difficult pitch to recover your par

Between the bunkers with a draw for your drive at the **seventh**
    tee
then a long iron or fairway wood fading in from the sea
don't attempt to shorten the hole by cutting the dog leg
better to shape your drive round the corner from your tee peg

Place your driver up the left at number **eight**
then a mid to long iron to the back will be great
cos if you don't make the green's top tier
the dreaded three putt is your biggest fear

The famous Turnberry lighthouse par three hole number **nine**
a fairway wood or long iron on the left edge with a fade will be
    fine
with the rocks on the left and bunker on the right
best to err towards the back as the front's too tight
for a hole which could make the world's top ten
how good will it feel to mark a three with your pen
then visit the Lighthouse for a refreshment or bite to eat
in Trumps Halfway House that's got the competition beat

On the right trap with your drive from the par five **tenth** tee
now decide where you want your second to be
lay up short of the bunker or go for the green
whether you can reach remains to be seen
an iron down the right is the safe shot to play
or a wood for the green which might go astray
it depends on your score and how you feel
whatever you do keep an even keel
Downwind err to the front and slightly right
beyond the green's too much of a fright
may be best to settle for a par
a birdie could be a step too far
indeed for some
but take it if it comes
as another day could be disaster
filling your opponents with laughter.

Mid to longish iron at the **eleventh** hole par three
drawing in from the right to avoid landing in the sea
best to be at the back so long as you're not too bold
it's tricky with a longish iron to get your ball to hold
the safe shot is landing to the right of the right hand trap
to be thrown onto the green behind if there's no mishap
and if you avoid a three putt you'll find
that elusive par three that was on your mind

Draw your drive on the right trap at the **twelfth** hole par four
if a long iron reaches the back who could ask for more
so long as you are able to cope
with this green's tricky slope

A driver on the left trap with a fade at the **thirteenth** hole
then a mid iron to the heart of the green won't be far from the
    flagpole
this green has no bunkers but sits on a plateau
and the ball will run off leaving a tricky pitch you know
so club selection and strike must be very precise
as missing this green won't cut any ice

Best at the par five **fourteenth** to play short of the right trap
    from the tee
then a second shot short of the left trap it should be
now with a shortish iron to pick
a chance of a birdie if you get close to the stick
Downwind, launch your drive over the left hand traps
now you can reach the green in two perhaps

Fifteen's a mid to longish iron drawing in from the right
holding the ball against the slope will keep a birdie in sight
as long as you are left with an uphill putt
with which to attack the cup

At **sixteen** drive down the middle of the fairway with a fade
leaves a mid to longish iron to the back left to be played
mustn't be short because of the high bank of the burn
go in there you won't know which way to turn
dropping under penalty leaves a pitch from a downhill slope
best get it right first time you hope

Down the left with your drive at this tough par four hole
    seventeen
then a long iron or fairway wood to make the green
if not then a straight forward pitch
can make a four if it goes without a hitch

Standing on the **eighteenth** tee look across the water to
    Ailsa Craig
and appreciate that this Scottish landscape only the creator
    could have made
look back inland towards the Trump Turnberry Hotel sitting
    high on the hilltop
and realise that you are going to play this final hole with the
    Hotel as your backdrop
so take a deep breath and savour the moment
taking it all in before making any movement
to lay up short of the left trap if you could
with a long iron or fairway wood
now a mid to longish iron coming in from the right

bunker short left makes the entrance tight
as you walk to the green soak up the atmosphere
and accept that your eye may cradle a tear
so when you pick your ball out of the cup
look all around you before looking up
at the Trump Turnberry Hotel in all its glory
then think of the words that best tell its story
but what words can you find when somehow
all you can say is WOW!

**There we have the course that made the duel in the sun
we may not be a Nicklaus or Watson but wasn't Turnberry
fun!**

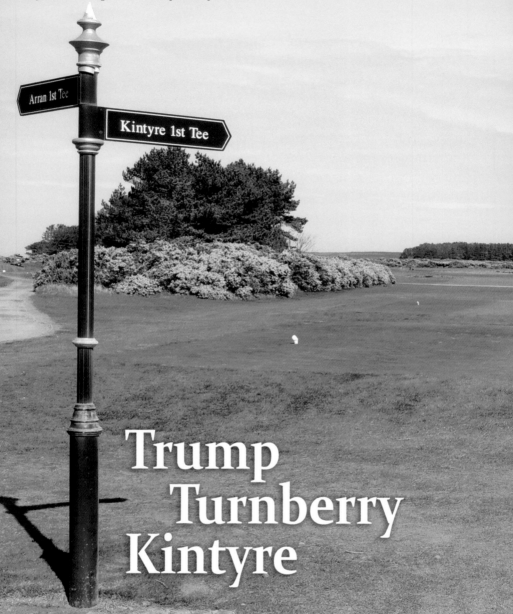

Trump
Turnberry
Kintyre

Let your Trump Turnberry
*   experience increase even higher*
play their other golf course
*   Trump Turnberry Kintyre*

At this **opening** par five drive on the left trap with a fade
from the back tee it's doubtful if this green can be made
in which case you must lay up short of the ditch
leaving yourself more than just a pitch
more like a mid iron left of centre dropping right
as the bunker on the right leaves that side tight
from a forward tee aim your second on the right trap drawing
    round
hit well there's a chance the green can be found
if not it can be just as much fun
making a birdie with a pitch and run

Second hole par three
back right of the green is the place to be
a longish iron left of centre fading in to the back
is the best way in which to attack

Fading inside the left traps with an iron or fairway wood
is the right approach for the **third** green if you could
a short iron fading in from the left side
can be the way to turn the tide

Hit a fairway wood on the left trap fading in
gives you the shortest route to the **fourth** pin
a mid iron over the left trap dropping right
should catch this green if it's got the right flight

Drive inside the left trap with a fade at the **fifth** hole par four
at this difficult hole to make a score
you need good position and distance from the tee
then a long iron inside the left trap with a fade and see
if the ball will roll to the right and be slightly long
with all the trouble at the front you want to be strong

Sixth hole par three
needs a long iron between you and me
hit inside the left trap fading round
for the back of this green to be found

On the end fir tree with a draw from the **seventh** tee
middle right of the fairway is where your drive should be
mid to short iron now to the left side
makes it more difficult for a birdie to hide

At the 309 yard par four hole number **eight**
reaching this green with one shot would be great
so launch a drive over the cairn and hope
that your ball gets the right bounce to give you some scope
to get down in two more
and help improve your score

Hit your drive at the par five **ninth** between the lighthouse and
    Ailsa Craig
it needs a big drive to have any chance of this green to be made
aim your second on the left trap drifting right
with any luck you might make it alright

From the **tenth** tee your drive should be inside the right trap
the ball will hold up against the slope if there's no mishap
now a long iron down the left side fading with ease
and this green and a par four can be achieved

A driver at **eleven** inside the left trap with a fade
will still leave a longish shot when all's been said
a mid to long iron on the left edge turning right
should hold the green if it's at the right height

The **twelfth** hole par three
could be a long iron or fairway wood you see
again hit down the left fading in
is the best way to get your ball near the tin

Drawing your drive down the right side at the **thirteenth** hole
will put you in good position to attack this flagpole
now a long iron or fairway wood
fading in from the left will be good

Inside the right trap with a draw for your drive at **fourteen**
will give you the best chance for this green to be seen
Smash a wood on the left trap with a fade
for a slim chance of the green to be made
if not keep your chins up
and hope for a pitch and a putt

Fade your drive inside the left trap at **fifteen**
to hit this green in two you'll have to be keen
a long iron or fairway wood drawing in from the right
bunker front left makes that approach too tight

Sixteenth hole par three
is only a mid to shortish iron from the tee
played to the centre back of the green
could produce a birdie if you know what I mean

Room on the left for your drive at the **seventeenth** hole par four
leaving the safest line to reach this green's core
then a long iron or fairway wood
drawing in from the right if you could

Down the left with a fade for your drive at the **eighteenth** par
     five
try to get past the right hand traps to keep your hopes alive
of reaching this green in two
a three wood drawing in from the right might do

**Did Trump Turnberry Kintyre
light your fire?**

Brunston Castle

*Whenever you want to escape
    life's hassle
hire a buggy and play golf at
    Brunston Castle*

Your **first** tee shot should be a three wood
on the left trap with a fade is good
putting you in position
to make the right decision
with a long iron down the right side
turning with a right to left slide
two putts and you are bound
to be pleased with your start to the round

A three wood again from the **second** tee
inside the left trap with a fade and see
a long iron for your second shot
inside the left trap for the green to be caught

An iron or fairway wood from the **third** tee
short right of the bunkers is the place to be
mid to long iron now to the pin
over the left trap fading in

Play short of the left trap at hole **four**
good position here can help your score
shortish iron to a narrow green
a bit of backspin needs to be seen

At the par three hole number **five**
best hit this green to keep your hopes alive
a long iron or fairway wood
to the left half of the green would be good

Go for a big drive down the middle with a fade at hole **six**
depending how far you then choose your sticks
a fairway wood over the left trap with a fade
has a chance of the green to be made
or a mid iron down the left hand side
then a wedge to the green perhaps settling for a five

Drive inside the right trap with a draw from the **seventh** tee
then a mid iron to the green it will be
drawing in from the right and slightly long
with a bunker front left short would be wrong

Longish iron at hole number **eight**
drawing in from the right would be great
two putts for a three
would be a good par here

Draw your driver inside the right trap at **nine**
getting past the bunkers will be fine
then a fairway wood inside the left trap fading in
not making a birdie at this par five would be a sin

Tenth tee is an iron down the right
then a short iron with a bit of bite
gives a chance of a three
then on to the next tee

Three wood at **eleven** down the left with a fade
leaves a shortish iron to the green to be played
left of centre and turning left to right
will hold the green if it's got enough height

Driver down the left from the **twelfth** tee
then a longish iron to the green it will be
coming in from the left with a left to right flight
it should make the green if you hit it right

Down the left again with your drive at **thirteen**
then a three wood drawing in from the right needs seen
it will take two good hits
to reach this green the way it sits

Fourteen is a long iron or fairway wood from the tee
still leaves only a shortish iron to the green you see
and if you find a flat lie
you can float it in nice and high

Hit a three wood at **fifteen** nice and straight
kept well away from the out of bounds golfers' hate
then a short iron left of centre drifting right
avoids the right side which is tight

Place your drive down the centre with a draw at **sixteen**
you are now in position to attack this green
a mid iron aimed at the greens heart
could just about rip this hole apart

At the **seventeenth** hole par three
a long iron coming in from the right it will be
erring slightly long
back of green is where you belong

Hole **eighteen** is a long iron or fairway wood
on the left trap with a fade is good
then a mid to long iron inside the left trap with a fade
gives the best chance for your score to be made

**Now that you and Brunston Castle are about to part
bet you're glad you hired the cart.**

Ballochmyle G.C.

In 1937 this Golf Club was founded
    at Ballochmyle
in the land o' Burns wid Rabbies face
    brek intae a smile
and wid he've gaun oot fer a gemme
    or wid he hae stay'd at hame

Would his **first** tee shot have been with a three wood
inside the trees on the left with a fade would be good
leaving only a wedge or a nine
to the front of the green would be fine

A driver at the **second** down the left with a fade
leaves only a shortish iron for this green to be made
bunker short left so err towards the back
best form of defence is attack

At the **third** hole par three
a long iron it must be
over the left trap fading in
is the way to approach the pin

Hit a three wood at the **fourth** from the tee
down the left with a fade and see
if a shortish iron to the left of the flag
can leave the right length of putt to bag

Drive down the right with a draw at hole **five**
chance of reaching this green in two shots from a good drive
with a long iron or wood for the front edge to be caught
parring this hole would mean a lot

The **sixth** hole par four
is a hole that can help your score
hit your driver down the left fading in trying to reach
this green in one shot would be a peach
approaching from the left hand side
there's nowhere for a birdie to hide

A three wood from the tee at the **seventh** hole
down the centre with a draw sounds very droll
but a shortish iron landing at the front to run on
can give a birdie chance to pounce upon

Inside the right trap with a draw at hole **eight**
right centre of fairway will be great
then a mid to short iron should be seen
turning in from the right of the green

Play an iron from the tee at **nine**
left centre of fairway is fine
leaves only a wedge to the pin
to leave yourself a putt to get in the tin
Downwind you can try and see
if you can reach the green from the tee

From the par four **tenth** tee
a driver it will be
drawing from the right hand trap
could reach the green perhaps

Take a fairway wood from the tee at **eleven**
finishing on the fairway would be heaven
to do so you'll need to hit it with a slice
missing the trees on the right would be nice
the bigger the slice the shorter the second shot will be
could be a shortish iron you see
playing a straight shot with an iron from the tee to the fairway
could leave you nearly 200 yards from the green by the way
which is a long iron in anyone's book
even longer if your tee shot turns into a hook
so if you can slice your tee shot high in the sky
the rewards on this dog leg are extremely high

Hit driver from the **twelfth** tee par four
up the left side some more
leaving only a pitch
a birdie should be a snitch

Big drive up the left again at **thirteen**
has a chance of reaching this green
if not a good pitch it will have to be
to deliver your birdie three

At the **fourteenth** hole par three
play a mid iron from the tee
inside the left trap fading round
for the back of the green to be found

Drive down the middle with a fade at the **fifteenth** par four
leaves only a wedge to the green to improve your score
best to err towards the back
so don't be afraid to attack

Draw your drive down the middle at **sixteen**
then a mid iron needs to be seen
erring to the left and a little short
bunker back right for your ball to be caught

Seventeenth par three hole
is a mid iron from the tee to the flagpole
inside the left trap and a little weak
avoids the out of bounds unless you hit it off the beak

A three wood down the middle at the **eighteenth** par five
too risky with the burn to go with your drive
then again for your second shot straight for the target
fading slightly right for the best view of the carpet
now a pitch to the pin
and try to get your putt in.

When Rabbie finish'd his gemme
wid he still remember'd her name
or wid he forgot'n fur a wee while
thaun bonie lass o' Ballochmyle.

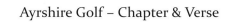

Here is one of the finest parkland
courses that you will play
in a while
let me guide you around Ayr Belleisle
Designed in 1927 by James Braid
it is a course which must be played

The **first** hole is a dog leg left par five
and from the tee requires a very good drive
drawing inside the end right hand tree
round the corner and see
if you can reach with a fairway wood
it depends on the wind but you should
drawing over the bunkers on the right
err long if you can as the entrance is tight

Second hole par five drive down the middle with a fade
then a fairway wood for the green to be made
aimed down the left fading in
being careful not to go beyond the pin
where the out of bounds lies close to the back
better to err short and left than to attack

At the uphill **third** hole par three
the green is surrounded by sand you see
at the front, left and back, but not to the right
so a longish iron to the right with a right to left flight
should be the way for the green to be caught
and avoid the dreaded bunker shot

Drive down the right with a draw at hole number **four**
then a mid to long iron fading in should help your score
provided you err slightly long
back right of green is where you belong

Fifth hole par four hit your drive up the centre
if you want a good score to enter
play a mid iron down the left edge fading right
is the way into this green try as you might

Inside the right trap with a draw at hole **six**
and you'll still have to give it big licks
with a long iron or fairway wood
over the right trap with a draw if you could

Mid iron at the **seventh** hole par three
middle right of green is the place to be
giving the best chance of holing a putt
especially if you're below the cup

Down the left with your drive at **eight**
left side of fairway will be great
leaving you only a wedge
if you are beyond the right hand hedge

Play a three wood up the left from the tee at **nine**
even in the semi rough will be fine
then a short iron to the middle right for some
and a possible birdie could be the outcome

At the **tenth** hole par three
a mid to long iron back right is the place to be
a good hole to escape with a par
can be a tricky hole by far

Big drive down the left at the par four **eleventh** hole
leaves a mid to long iron again which sounds very droll
on the left trap with a fade
for a tough par four when all's been said

On the left trap with a fade at the par four **twelfth** hole
another tough hole to get near the flagpole
play a mid to long iron on the left edge fading in
cos of a huge tree on the right shielding the pin

A three wood from the tee at hole **thirteen**
cos it's a tough shot up the hill for this green to be seen
having laid up back from the slope, play a fairway wood
to the back of the green will be good
with two bunkers at the front making the entrance tight
and no trouble at the back erring long is right

Hit a long iron with a draw at the **fourteenth** par three
middle left of centre is the place to be
with the ground on the right all falling away
up the left is the way to play

Par five **fifteenth**, drive on the left trap with a fade
now a fairway wood drawing from the right side can be played
even if you're not accurate enough
you can still pitch and putt from the semi rough

Unless downwind, lay up with a fairway wood at **sixteen** short
    of the burn
then a longish iron on the left trap with a fade and a bit of run
if you can escape with a par four
you can be really pleased with your score
Downwind, you can carry the burn with your drive
leaving only a shortish iron from a great height to dive
onto the green giving a much better chance
for your score to be enhanced

The **seventeenth** hole par three
needs a crisp mid iron to the centre of the green you see
as it's surrounded by sand with no safe shot
and the burn at the front if you fall short
if you're concerned that your ball may be caught
you must step up to the mark and hit a good shot

Again unless downwind, play a three wood from the
    eighteenth tee
short of the middle bunkers you want to be
then a three wood down the middle with a fade
to approach from the right for the green to be made
now it's just a wedge to the flag
and a chance of a birdie to bag
downwind, a big drive can carry the traps
and reach this par five in two shots perhaps
a fairway wood turning in from the right
can land on the carpet if it's at the right height
and with two putts for a birdie four
further improve your score

Being a parkland course
with not a lot of run of course
perhaps Belleisle's greatest strength
is that it plays its full length
and you have to drive the ball really well from the tee
to reach many of these greens you see
therein lies your biggest test
that you have to play your best
to have a chance of scoring well
in that only you can tell.

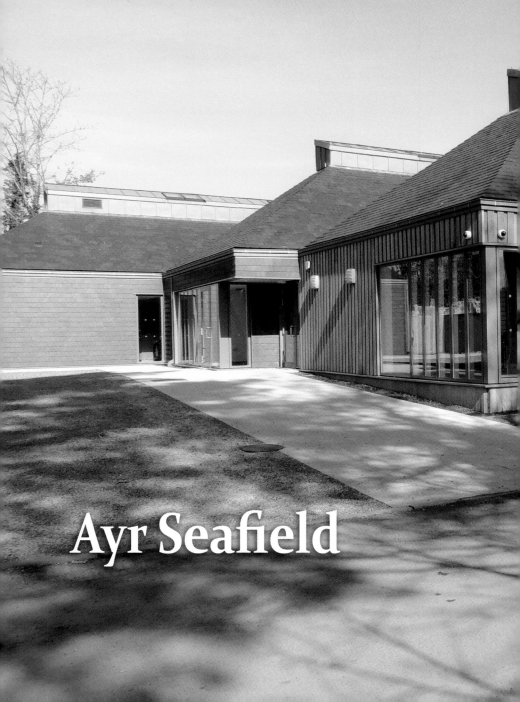

Ayr Seafield

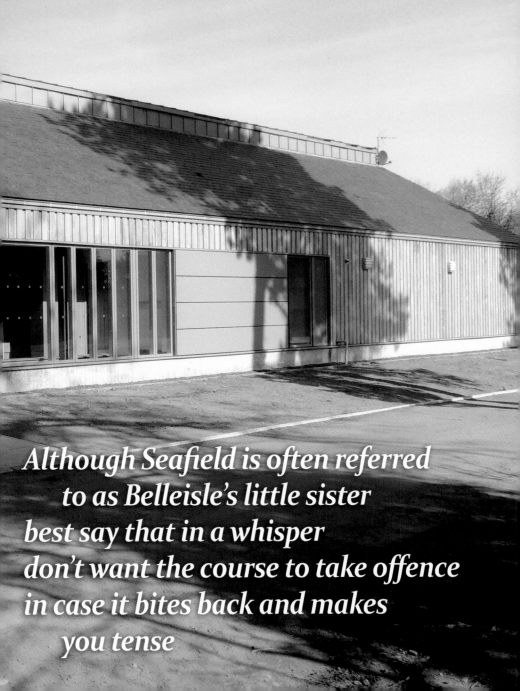

*Although Seafield is often referred
    to as Belleisle's little sister
best say that in a whisper
don't want the course to take offence
in case it bites back and makes
    you tense*

Your **opening** hole is a tough par three
requiring a really good shot from the back tee
a long iron or fairway wood
on the left edge with a fade will be good
if you can scramble your par
you'll start off on the right foot by far
playing from the front tee on the green side of the stream
you can reach with a mid iron if you see what I mean

Draw a three wood from the right at the par four **second** hole
now a mid to short iron to reach the flagpole
Coming in on the right side with a right to left turn
should keep you well away from the burn

A longish iron at the **third** hole par three from the tee
inside the left trap with a fade it should be
turning in with its left to right flight
should land on the green and hold with some bite

At the fourth tee par **four** play your number one wood
fading over the path and short of the traps if you could
now a mid iron to the back of the green will suffice
and no more than two putts would be nice

Fading your drive on the left edge just might
reach this **fifth** green if you can hit it right
better to be in the right hand bunker than in the trees
so err if anything to the right if you please

Go for a big drive at the **sixth** fading to the target
it'll take a big shot to reach the carpet
but if you don't, making a birdie should still be a snitch
provided you can play a good pitch

There are two ways of playing the **seventh** hole par four
and a lot depends on the state of your score
A driver over the left trap fading in
can leave a nice short approach to the pin
or an iron placed short right of the trap
leaves only about an eight or nine iron to rap
which would be the safe way to play
and depends entirely on your score I'd say

Drive between the middle and right traps at hole **eight**
anywhere on the fairway will be great
leaving a mid to shortish iron to the stick
two bunkers at the front one at the back so take your pick

Play a long iron or fairway wood at the par three hole **nine**
drawing in from the right side should be fine
two putting for a par three
would be good enough for me

From the **tenth** tee play a three wood at this shortish par four
laying up can open rather than close the door
a full shot for your second makes it easier to play short of the wall
landing front right of the green would make your tee shot the
    right call

Driving down the right side from the par four **eleventh** tee
opens up the approach to the green you see
pitching between the traps with a clear sight of the flag
gives you a chance of a birdie to bag

Hitting down the right again at the **twelfth** hole par four
so long as you don't hook it you can give it a bit more
and you'll only need a wedge
if you are level with the gap in the hedge

A big drive down the right at the par four hole **thirteen**
can leave a good mid iron to the green
play to the left edge and a little short
don't want the out of bounds caught

Aim your drive on the right trap from the **fourteenth** tee par
    four
with the right draw this green can be reached right to its core
be careful not to overdo the draw and miss to the left of it
better if anything to err to the right a little bit

At the **fifteenth** hole par three
play a mid iron from the tee cos you see
this is a green you must attack
with the water at the front you're safer at the back

The **sixteenth** par four goes back up the slope
drive on the left trap with a fade and a lot of hope
you'll have a good chance of making a three
if you keep up the left from the tee

Three wood from the par four **seventeenth** tee hit out to the
    right
with a left to right flight
because of a large tree shielding the left side of the dance floor
you have to approach from the right a bit more

Hit your three wood again at the **eighteenth** slightly left fading
    round
for the middle of this par four fairway to be found
then a wedge coming in from the right
will kick down to the pin without much of a fight

Now you've played Belleisle's little sister
you wouldn't call her a 'B' lister
shorter yes but no easy touch
and some may say they enjoyed it just as much.

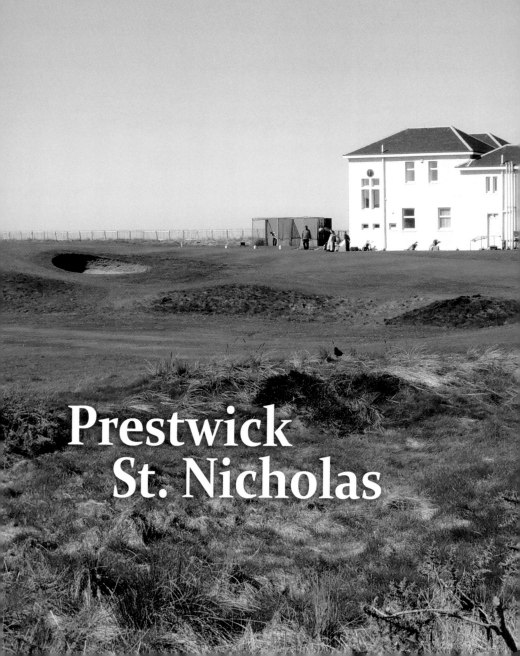

Prestwick
St. Nicholas

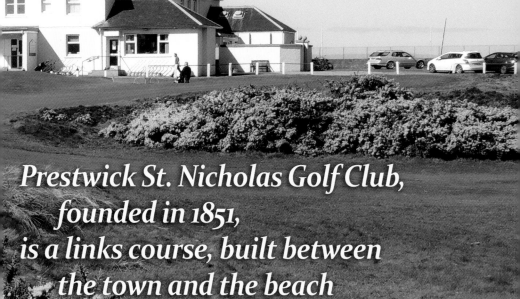

Prestwick St. Nicholas Golf Club,
*   founded in 1851,*
is a links course, built between
*   the town and the beach*
it has a Railway Station and an Airport
both within easy reach

Play an iron from the **first** tee inside the right trap drawing round
better to be slightly short and between the traps with the fairway
    found
you are now only left with a seven or an eight
back of the green will accommodate

The **second** hole par three
is a longish iron from the tee
played to the left edge turning right
to a two tier green err long to give your putter some respite

From the **third** tee play an iron or fairway wood
to the right side of fairway if you could
giving you the best line to attack the flag
and a better chance of a birdie to bag

Drive slightly left at hole number **four**
leaving you the safest line in to reach the green's core
a mid to longish iron coming in from the right
err to the front as the out of bounds at the back is tight

Hit your driver over the right trap at hole **five**
you'll be left with only a mid iron off a good drive
erring to the front and slightly right
as at the back the ball will run off as it might

An iron or fairway wood from the tee at the **sixth** hole par four
another hole where you can improve your score
provided you avoid the trouble by hitting it left from the tee
then it's only a wedge to the green you see

Big drive at **seven** down the left with a fade
if you're over the ridge then the green can be made
a longish iron coming in from the right
it runs off at the back so erring short is bright

Three wood from the tee at hole **eight**
up the left edge of fairway will be great
a short iron now to the left side of the pin
hit it crisply if you want some backspin

It's an iron from the tee at **nine**
short of the right hand trap will be fine
then a wedge coming in from the right
might bag a birdie alright

Mid iron at the **tenth** hole par three
fading in from the left it must be
you want to err towards the back
but not so much that you can attack

Down the left with a big drive at the **eleventh** hole par five
chance of reaching this green from a good drive
then a three wood up the right to kick in
could finish up close to this pin

A long iron at the **twelfth** hole par three
hit up to the right and see
if it will kick down towards the target
to finish on the middle of the carpet

Up to the right with your drive at hole **thirteen**
if you're past the traps on the left this green can be seen
with a long iron or fairway wood
on the left trap with a fade would be good

With your tee shot at **fourteen** aim on the left trap with a fade
it'll take a long iron to reach this green when all's been said
hit on the left trap turning right and slightly short
all you want is a safe par to be got

On the middle trap with a draw for your drive at **fifteen**
with any luck that will be enough to reach this green
if not you'll just have to make it up
with a pitch and a putt

Tee off at **sixteen** with a long iron or fairway wood
left of centre would be good
leaving you with only an eight or a nine
back of green will be fine

At the **seventeenth** take your driver on the tee
on the left trap with a fade and see
if you can reach the green's apron
if not you'll just have to pitch on

Fairway wood at the **last**
and see if you can guide the ball past
between the clubhouse and the trap
if you do you'll get a clap

Now you've played the course and seen the clubhouse
there is one thing you should remember
not many Clubs can boast
Old Tom Morris as a founder member.

Prestwick
St. Cuthbert

Prestwick St. Cuthbert is a tree
    lined course
with a number of holes which dogleg
so position is all important
when you sit your ball on the tee peg

Your **opening** tee shot should be with a three wood
right of centre with a draw is good
now a shortish iron to the right half of the green
two putts and a steady par can be seen

Inside the right trap with your drive at the **second** with a fade
then a mid iron to the right half of the green needs made
two putting for another steady four
will consolidate your score

Driver down the middle with a fade at the **third** hole par five
now a long iron or fairway wood can reach this green off a good
    drive
aiming your second shot on the left trap with a fade just might
produce a birdie if you can hit it right

Driving between the bunkers at the **fourth** with a draw is the
    shot
then a long iron or fairway wood for this green to be caught
aimed inside the left trap with a fade will be fine
you would take a four here every time

Play short of the right bunker at the **fifth** with a fairway wood
leaves only a short iron to the green if you could
coming in from the right hand side
with a slight right to left slide

A fairway wood from the tee at the par four **sixth** hole
now here is a hole to lift your soul
you are left with a shortish shot to the pin
which you can attack using backspin

The **seventh** hole par three
is well bunkered as you'll see
but a mid to long iron drawing in from the right
can open up this green with a little bite

At the par five **eighth** hole
laying up from the tee is a bit droll
and although carrying the ditch takes a big hit
it's worth it so go for it!
cos a fairway wood on the left trap fading in
can yield a birdie if you get two putts in the tin

On the par three hole number **nine**
a longish iron inside the left trap with a fade is fine
and although finishing on the top tier is where you want to be
the important thing is to score no more than a three

Take a driver on the par four **tenth** tee 335 yards
a good drive here can really help your card
aim on the left trap with a fade and see
how close to the green you will be
if you don't reach it can still be fun
to hit it stiff with a pitch and run

Hit your driver up the left at the **eleventh** hole with a fade
you'll still have a long shot left when all's been said
a fairway wood on the left trap drifting in
can reach this green if not the pin

Fairway wood or iron from the **twelfth** tee
down the middle with a draw and see
a full shot with a short iron land on the green and stop
cos cutting the corner from the tee's not much cop

Between the bunkers with a fade for your drive at **thirteen**
now fade a long iron inside the left trap to the green
concentrate on two putting before
thinking about the rest of your score

Long iron at the **fourteenth** hole par three
inside the left trap with a fade it will be
if your ball can finish on the green back right
with the trouble at the front big is bright

Draw your drive at **fifteen** down the right
it's now only a shortish iron to a green which is tight
with the trouble at the front and not at the back
feel safe to attack

Fade a drive inside the right trap at the **sixteenth** par four
a short iron again to the green can open the door
inside the right trap turning in from the right
you can make the top tier if it's at the right height

Mid to long iron at the **seventeenth** par three
inside the left trap with a fade is the key
to giving you the chance of holing the putt
providing you left it below the cup

Down the centre with a fade for your drive from the
    eighteenth tee
then a fairway wood to the green it needs to be
don't worry if it doesn't get up
you can still make four with a pitch and putt

**There ends your experience of Prestwick St. Cuthbert
the fact you'll be back is a dead cert.**

WHITE MARKER
Medal Tee - S.S.S. 73

YELLOW BOXE
Tee of the day - S.S.S. 7

RED MARKERS
Ladies Tee - S.S.S. 75

White markers may only
be used by prior arrangeme

Troon
Lochgreen

Remember Folks,
Your place on the golf
course is immediately
behind the game in
front, not immediately
in front of the
game behind!

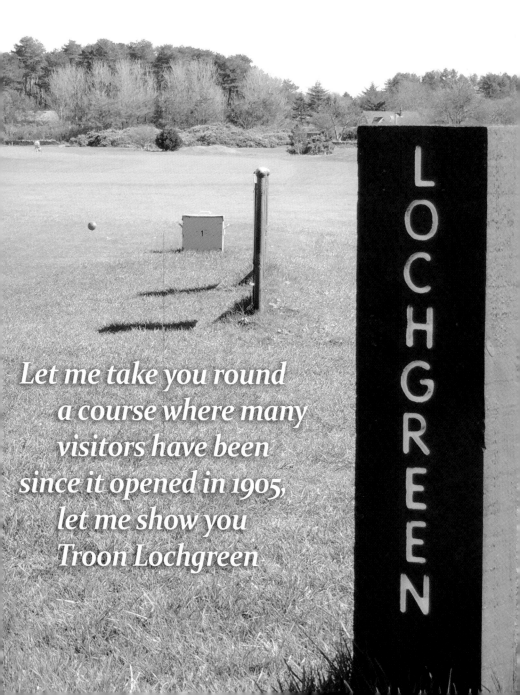

Let me take you round
a course where many
visitors have been
since it opened in 1905,
let me show you
Troon Lochgreen

Your **first** hole is a long par four and wide open
so open your shoulders and go for the big drive that you've
    been hoping
aim between the bunkers and draw it round the bend
you've now got a long iron or fairway wood with which
    to contend
aim your second on the right trap and draw it landing short
    to run on
get down in two and you have the foundation of a score
    to build upon

Second hole is a straight par five
aim inside the right hand trap and draw your drive
now a long iron or fairway wood on the left trap fading right
gives the best chance of reaching in two with the right flight

The **third** is another par five you can reach in two
drive on the right hand trap for the best view
for a long iron or fairway wood
to carry the greenside bunkers if you could
but not too much cos if you go too far
you could end up hitting a car

Unless downwind at the **fourth** lay up short of the bunkers
    and slope
leaving only a wedge shot to hit close you hope
downwind you can take the driver and see
if you can drive the green from the tee

Play a three wood at the **fifth** on the left trap with a fade
then for the green to be made
requires a mid to longish iron drawing in from the right side
err long as the entrance is tight I can confide

Par three **sixth** is a longish iron on the tee
aimed on the left hand trap with a fade it should be
if you can play it long to the right
as the bunkers at the front are tight

Hole **seven** is a straight par five which can be caught
in two good shots then you ought
to improve your score
by making a four

Launch a drive at the par four **eighth** for the green
where it remains to be seen
if you can pick a stroke up
with a pitch and a putt

At the par four hole number **nine**
all will be fine
drawing your drive from the tee
over the right hand trap you see
then a mid to long iron safely on to the carpet
but erring back left of the target

The par three **tenth** is a long iron or fairway wood
on the left trap with a fade would be good
played to the back right
gives the best chance of a par with hindsight

Drive over the right trap at the **eleventh** par four
then a mid iron back right could help your score
with another par to help consolidate
now wouldn't that be great

Twelfth hole par four drive down the right
from where you just might
play a mid iron back right
as the front is tight

Up the left with your drive at the **thirteenth** tee
then you can see
if a birdie it will be
by getting down in three

From the **fourteenth** tee drive down the left side drawing
    round
a big drive here and the green could be found
but if you don't get up
you can still make birdie with a pitch and a putt

At the **fifteenth** hole par three
it will need to be
a fairway wood on the left traps fading in
takes a good shot to get near this pin

Hit your drive at the par five **sixteenth** down the left side
    if you could
then you can reach the green with a big three wood
coming in from the left if you can
provided the ball ran

Lay up at the **seventeenth** short of the bunkers and wall
then a shortish iron back right's your call
where you might just hole a putt
with a bit of luck

The par five **eighteenth** go for a big drive long and straight
and hope it's not too late
to improve your score
cos you can do no more
than give it your best
and be up for the test
so play a fairway wood drawing in from the right trap
making an eagle or birdie would deserve a clap.

Now you can say you have been
and played Troon's Lochgreen.

Troon Darley

WHITE MARKERS
Medal Tee - S.S.S. 71

YELLOW BOXES
Tee of the day - S.S.S. 70

RED MARKERS
Ladies Tee - S.S.S. 73

White markers may only
be used by prior arrangement.

Remember Folks,
Your place on the golf
course is immediately
behind the game in
front, not immediately
in front of the

*Here is a course which opened
in 1905, where you'll hardly
curb your enthusiasm around
Troon Darley*

This is a superb **opening** tee shot
with little rough one which you ought
at this opening par five let rip
and give it a big hit
now a long iron or fairway wood
on the right trap with a draw if you could
landing short to run on to the green
could a birdie this early be seen

Your **second** tee shot is with a three wood
to the bottom of the slope would be good
from where a mid to short iron left of the pin
could give a chance of a putt to get in

The **third** tee we're going for a big drive
we're rocking and rolling and going for a jive
towards the left side of the green
a pitch and putt gives us the best start there's been

At the **fourth** hole par three
we're hoping to see
a mid iron left of centre
and a solid par to enter

From the **fifth** tee drive up the right hand side
then a longish iron between the bunkers with a right
    slide
finishing on the green back right
if you give it the correct flight

Drive down the right side at hole **six**
giving it big licks
same again for your second shot
although the green may not be caught
a nice pitch and putt
could chalk another birdie up

On the **seventh** tee
play a three wood on the left trap you can see
then a shortish iron beyond the flag
the troubles at the front and there's a birdie to bag

A three wood from the tee at **eight**
short of the slope will be great
mid to short iron to the back you should err
bunkers at front so back you prefer

Par three hole number **nine**
will be fine
with a mid iron which might
carry the front left of the green which is tight

Fairway wood from the tee at **ten**
you're only left with a wedge then
with no trouble at the back
so you can safely attack

Driver at **eleven** down the right
bunkers at front make the entrance tight
so mid iron to long
you want to err strong

The par three hole number **twelve**
into the bag for a mid iron you must delve
hit straight and long
back of green is where you belong

Play a fairway wood from the tee at **thirteen**
laying up short of the stream
then a long iron or fairway wood
to the right side of green if you could

Drive to the right at **fourteen**
then a mid iron to the right side of green
avoiding the burn
appearing at every turn

At the **fifteenth** take your three wood from the tee
short right of the slope is the place to be
then a shortish iron with plenty height
cos when it hits the green you want it to bite

A mid iron at the **sixteenth** hole
to the back right of the flagpole
two putts for a three
is the way it should be

Down the left with your drive at the **seventeenth** par four
leaving a shortish shot to help your score
cos it's only a wedge
if you're past the gap in the hedge

Big drive down the left at par five **eighteenth** fairway
leaves a long iron or fairway wood to the green I'd say
aim on the left trap with a fade
and another birdie could be made.

Now you'll want to parley
if you scored round Darley.

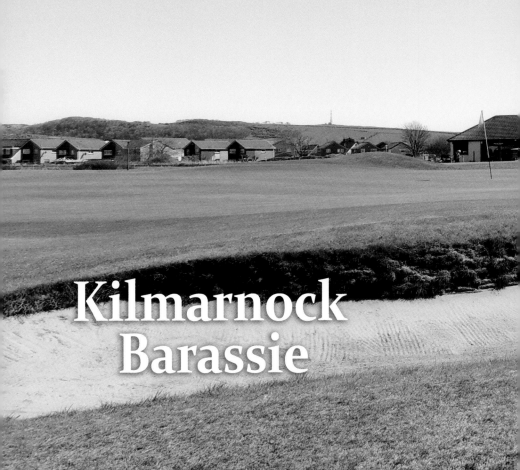

Kilmarnock
Barassie

*If ever an opening hole gave you
    the chance to start with a birdie
that would be the par five first hole
    at Kilmarnock Barassie
Founded in 1887 and moving
    to Barassie in 1894
with predominately Kilmarnock
    residents at it's core*

Aim your **first** drive at the second left hand bunker with a fade
finish on the fairway and this green can be made
with a long iron or fairway wood
on the left edge of the green would be good
where the ball will run down to the right
giving you the chance of an eagle as you might

Play short of the right hand bunker with an iron or fairway wood
at the **second** hole par four if you could
leaving a mid iron and a straight shot
for this tricky green to be caught

Drive down the left with a fade at the par four **third**
not a hole likely to give up a bird
but keeping well away from the out of bounds on the right
the wall's too close making that side tight
then a mid to longish iron to the left side of the target
where the ball will kick down to finish on the carpet

At the **fourth** hole par three
a mid to longish iron with a fade and see
if the ball can hold the green and not revolve
down the slope getting the burn involved

Hit your drive towards the right trap at the **fifth** hole par four
then a longish iron fading in to reach the green's core
if you can two putt for a par
it will be a good score by far

The **sixth** hole par three
a mid iron inside the right trap with a draw it will be
where the green will gather your ball
making your club selection the right call

Place your drive down the centre with a fade at the **seventh**
    hole
hitting this green in two shots is good for the soul
a longish iron drawing in from the right side
two bunkers on the left makes that side a bumpy ride

Down the right with a draw for your drive at hole **eight**
then a three wood coming in from the left will be great
reducing this par five to two shots
could be worth the gamble and cost

Aim your drive at the right trap at **nine**
so long as you are short you'll be fine
only a mid iron to the back left of the pin
then it's up to you to get the putt in the tin

A three wood inside the right trap at the **tenth** hole par four
a hole where you can improve your score
now a short iron drawing in from the right side
the ball will roll to where a birdie can't hide

From the **eleventh** tee play your three wood again out to the
    right
bunkers on the left make that approach tight
then a mid iron to the green
where there are no bunkers to be seen

Lay up short of the right hand trap if you could
from the **twelfth** tee with a fairway wood
then another fairway wood down the right side and a little short
now a nice pitch can give a birdie if you're hot

An iron or fairway wood at **thirteen** from the tee
aimed at the second left hand trap you can see
just a shortish iron to the front erring short
not wanting the burn at the back to be caught

At the par three **fourteenth** hole
hit a longish iron to the flagpole
try and stay below the cup
to leave you with an uphill putt

Left of centre with your drive at **fifteen** kicking to the right
then a longish iron fading from the left could excite
by landing on a bowl shaped green which gathers the ball
might not leave you much of a putt at all

Fade your drive down the left at the **sixteenth** hole par five
then a wood drawing from the right can reach off a good drive
two putts on a long green breaking right to left
can yield a birdie with a touch that is deft

Draw your drive on the second right hand traps turning in
leaving a mid to shortish iron to the pin
at **seventeen** drawing in from the right
your ball should hold the narrow green if it's at the right height

Hit a three wood from the **eighteenth** tee
on the middle bunker in the distance you see
then a shortish iron to the right side
where the ball kicking left will fill you with pride

**Your pleasure of playing Kilmarnock Barassie
depends on keeping out of the heather
if you can manage to do that
you won't reach the end of your tether.**

Western Gailes

*Founded in 1897, Western Gailes
is a superb seaside links on
the Ayrshire coast
One of the best seaside links in the
country could be their boast*

Your **first** hole for big hitters can be reached in one shot
but with the humps and bumps and bounces deep rough can
    be caught
better to play an iron from the tee
down the left hand side is the place to be
you then have a nice wedge shot from a flat lie
landing on a flat green chance of a birdie is high

A three wood at the **second** drawing from the right hand trap
will leave you sitting pretty to land your second on its lap
a longish iron on the left trap fading in
should be the way to approach this pin

Down the left at the **third** fading your three wood
now an eight or nine should be good
left of centre is your line
one or two putts will be fine

Between the bunkers with a three wood at **four** and short
    of the slope
then a strong mid iron to the back of the green you hope
from where two putts will suffice
making another par will be nice

Drive down the right with a draw at **five**
then a good long iron or fairway wood will keep your
    hopes alive
of continuing your run
with more pars to come

Hole **six** par five needs a big drive down the right
the opening to this green is tight
shielded by a bunker on top of a mound
best to use the contours of the ground
and come in from the right side
the wind from the sea will help the ball slide
towards the target
maybe creeping on to the carpet

Best way for the par three **seventh** green to be made
is with a long iron and a fade
if you can avoid the sand and the hollows you'll see
if you can salvage a three

Hit your drive down the right at **eight**
hitting the fairway will be great
you'll be left with an eight or nine
short of the pin will be fine

Three wood down the right at **nine**
a wedge coming in from the left is the line
played up to the back left of the dance floor
could have a birdie knocking at the door

Play down the right at the **tenth** with your three wood
anywhere on the fairway is good
only a wedge left to the flag
for another possible birdie to bag

Drive down the left at the **eleventh** with a fade
still leaves a tough second shot with a long iron when all's
    been said
aim at the right hand trap with a draw
hitting this green will be braw

Another tough drive down the left at hole **twelve**
and into your bag for another long iron you must delve
try to finish at the back right
as the entrance to this green's tight

Thirteenth green is surrounded by sand
so if you want a hand
err middle back half
and don't do anything daft

Aim on the left trap at the par five **fourteenth** with a three wood
then another three wood over the left traps is good
now a wedge to the back right
will stop well if it's at the right height

Fifteen is a tough par three
much tougher than people see
it takes a long iron to the middle front
a two here would be worth a punt

A three wood at **sixteen** middle right
then a long iron to a green that's tight
take plenty of club to get over the burn
even then there's trouble at every turn

The **seventeenth** is a tough par four
which can ruin many a good score
with the railway line all the way down the right
you have to be prepared to put up a good fight
it requires a good drive on the left hand trap with a fade
you need to be past the bunker for the green to be made
now a long iron over the mound coming in from the left side
keeping left to avoid the sand where your ball can hide
a chip and a putt is your best chance to save
dropping a stroke if your ball misbehaves

Now the **eighteenth** tee and your three wood
on the left hand bunker with a fade is good
then a mid iron to the front left is ideal
hole the putt and you've sealed the real deal.

**You now have many tales
to tell about Western Gailes.**

Dundonald Links

Dundonald Links is a relatively
*   new course*
using the name and on the site
*   of an old one*
it is a course which will surprise
*   and delight*
and if you are playing golf in Ayrshire
*   you must come*

As this **opening** tee shot needs to finish slightly right
aiming your drive on the left trap with a fade would be bright
the same shot with a long iron over the left trap to the green
and for this round you'll have set the scene

Hit three wood at the **second** on the left trap fading in
leaves only a mid to shortish iron to attack the pin
erring slightly right and long
puts your ball where you belong

On the left trap with a fade at the par five **third**
could give you a good chance of bagging a bird
finishing between the trap and the ditch
your second shot can reach if it goes without a hitch
if it doesn't all is not yet lost
a pitch and a putt can retrieve the cost

Play a long iron or fairway wood at the par three hole number **four**
finishing on the front half of the green can help your score
by leaving you an uphill putt
with which to attack the cup

Draw a driver inside the right trap at the par five **fifth** tee
then a chance of reaching the green with fairway wood number
    three
if not, a straight forward pitch and run
could yield a birdie for some

Hitting a mid iron to the right side of the green at the par three
    sixth hole
avoids the trouble on the left which could really take its toll
and leave you with a putt to lag
across the green to the flag

A three wood from the **seventh** tee
aimed at the middle bunker you see
leaves a mid iron to the back right of the green
avoiding the trap front left where you might have been

Aim at the left trap with a three wood at hole **eight**
fading to the middle of the fairway would be great
then a mid iron to the back of the green
is where you want your ball to be seen

Take a three wood again at **nine**
over the middle bunker will be fine
now a shortish iron to the back of the green
avoiding the bunkers at the front, and the stream

At the **tenth** take a driver on the tee
aim down the centre and hitting a draw is the key
which leaves a long iron or fairway wood
turning in from the right is good

A shortish iron at hole number **eleven**
hitting the green would be heaven
beware of bunkers both short and beyond the green
beyond lies a bunker which can't be seen
a small pot bunker which is quite deep
with a face that is steep
its distance to the flag is tricky
and the grass is not very sticky
if you don't get out far enough the ball comes back to the
    sand
too far, you're in sand at the front, in need of a helping hand
so club selection on the tee is vital
for this hole to be delightful

Drive from the **twelfth** tee
inside the left trap with a fade it will be
then a short iron hit into the greens slope
leaving an uphill putt you hope

Three wood from the tee at **thirteen**
leaves a shortish iron to the green
a shot with which you must be bold
as the ball will screw back threefold

Fourteen's a big drive down the left fading round
and this green with your second shot can be found
a big three wood turning left to right
can unlock a green which is tight
and yield a birdie four
to help improve your score

Long iron or fairway wood at the **fifteenth** hole par three
coming in from the right side it will be
the green will gather your ball towards the centre
leaving you with a putt for a birdie to enter

Sixteen's a driver on the left trap turning right
leaves a long iron or fairway wood to be hit light
aim on the greenside bunker but come up short
you don't want your ball to be caught
and try to get down from the front in two more
to protect your score

Draw a three wood down the right at the **seventeenth** hole par four
leaves a mid iron to the green and not a lot more
coming in from the right and slightly long
bunker short left so best to be strong

At **eighteen** drive on the left trap with a fade
unless downwind this green can't be made
so lay up with an iron over the bunkers on the right
then a short iron to the green with plenty of bite.

**So there we have Dundonald Links
a course worth playing methinks.**

Glasgow Gailes

*Opened in 1892 the game of golf
never fails
to impress round Glasgow Gailes*

On the **first** tee take an iron or fairway wood
down the left hand side is good
stay away from the right to avoid wailing sounds
should your ball go out of bounds
you now have a short iron albeit a full shot
with the only trouble being short
and played to a flat green
a chance of a birdie could be seen

Play an iron off the **second** tee
middle right of centre is the place to be
leaving a short iron to the front right
careful not to spin off as the ball will bite

Three wood from the **third** tee
aimed at the left hand bunker you see
then a mid to long iron to the back left of target
should see you safely on to the carpet

Drive down the right with a draw at **four**
which is a tough hole to make a score
then a long iron towards the left bunker with a fade
will give you a chance of a four to be made

At the **fifth** drive towards the right hand trap
if you ever reach it you'll deserve a clap
then a three wood aimed down the right side
if you don't reach there's just a pitch to fill you with pride

A mid iron at the **sixth** played with precision
should substantiate your decision
to attack the flag
cos there's a birdie to be had

Hit a three wood at **seven**
left of centre is heaven
now a mid to long iron to the back of green
avoids the traps where others have been

An iron from the tee at **eight**
right of centre is great
leaves a full shot with a short stick
middle of green should be your pick

Place an iron at **nine**
short of the ridge will be fine
leaving a full shot to the flag
and another possible birdie to bag

Down the right with your drive at **ten**
a mid iron front left of green then
two putt for a four
and you'll have made a good score

Driver at **eleven** down the right
and a mid to long iron just might
give you the chance of a birdie and par putt
so long as your second shot is up

Longish iron from the **twelfth** tee
fading in from the left at this par three
will give you the best chance by far
of walking away with a par

Lay up with an iron from the tee at the **thirteenth** hole
so you are not too close to the flagpole
leaving you with a full shot
and a possible birdie to be caught

Fourteenth is your three wood
drawing from the right hand bunker is good
play it again down the right side of fairway
leaving only a wedge to play

Mid iron at **fifteen** fading in
to the front middle of green and short of the pin
leaving two putts for a par three
an acceptable result you'll agree

Sixteen's a drive on the left hand bunker with a fade
still leaves a long iron to the green when all's been said
fading in from the left hand trap
should catch this green if there's no mishap

A three wood down the left at **seventeen**
leaves a shortish iron to the green
drawing in from the right
makes this green a pretty sight

Drive down the right at the **eighteenth** fairway
leaving a mid iron to the green I'd say
aiming for the greens centre
could yield another par to enter.

**If ever there was a course to take the wind out of your sails
between the weather and the heather that would be
  Glasgow Gailes.**

Irvine Bogside

*Join me while I give you a guide
round Irvine Golf Club Bogside
1887 was the year it was founded
and the three 'R's' have it surrounded
(railway, river, racecourse)*

Your **opening** hole is a tough par four
but unless downwind if you want to score
best play it as a five
and keep your hopes alive
Take a three wood from the tee
because as you'll see
there's lots of room on the right
but going left will give you a fright
so aim right and lay up short of the slope
for a flat lie you hope
then a five wood to give you some height
to clear the slope and aim slightly right
carrying the fairway bunker's your aim
then a nice pitch and your par you could claim
Downwind with a driver you can carry the hill
and you'll feel as though you've taken a Popeye pill
aided by the downslope you'll only have a short iron to play
much to your opponent's dismay

The **second** needs a good drive early in the round
then a long iron or wood catching the downslope of the mound
shooting you towards the green
gaining a stroke remains to be seen

An iron or fairway wood at the **third**
leaves a wedge and a putt for your bird
but if it spins off the front into the gully
take your putter don't pitch in a hurry
all that you want to be seen
is your ball back on the green
not facing the same shot again
and again and again

A four iron at the railway hole **fourth**
leaves another wedge of course
laying up lets you see the full green
and easier to avoid where the trains have been

Unless downwind, play the **fifth** the same as number four
if you trust your wedge you can lower your score
Downwind you can gamble or play safe
it takes a big drive to carry Sandface

Hole **six** is downhill close to the waters edge
and is not a hole normally reached with a wedge
A three wood played left can give you a good view
of the green from up high which you can reach in two
it will take a long iron played slightly left and short
erring on the side of caution not wanting the river caught
this leaves a short chip with no bunkers to cross
and playing away from water in which your ball could be lost
so now a good putt can rescue your par
and let you concentrate on improving your score by far

Play a three wood at the **seventh** alongside the final furlong
    of the Racecourse
you're going back up the hill and don't want the slope caught
    of course
now choose between a wedge or a nine
whichever you play will finish just fine
the green slopes right to left and back to front
if you choose the wedge you can give it a dunt
if you take the nine and hit it a little big
it'll spin back off the slope if you give it a dig
Probably best to make sure you are up
if you want to get your ball in THE CUP!

Par three **eighth** is surrounded by sand
so you need to hit the green as planned
and have a stab at a birdie if not settle for a par three
could have been worse trust me

Racecourse hole number **nine** drive down the left in front
     of the Grandstand
then a long iron or wood fading in from the left you
     understand
to avoid the greenside bunker on the right
which makes the entrance from that side tight

On the **tenth** tee take a one iron or three wood
leaving a shortish iron dropping slightly right if you could
cos the green slopes right to left and front to back
and is not a green to attack
but to land on the front fringe rolling down and hopefully lag
somewhere close enough to the flag

Tee shot at **eleven** can be drawn around the sand
leaving only a mid iron on a narrow green to land
if you want a birdie favour the left side of the pin
the ground falls away to the right and you would have to chip in

A three wood at **twelve** hit out to the right
then a wedge played short running downhill as it might
cos the fairway and green slope severely front to back
making it difficult to attack
especially as the shot is blind
and having to land well short you'll find
to avoid going through
so it's up to you

At the bell hole **thirteenth** take the three wood before
a long iron slightly right to kick down some more
hopefully the slope of the green will leave your ball below the pin
to give you a better chance of getting your putt in the tin

Three wood again at **fourteen** 'The Specs' down the right side
then a short iron to the right again depending where the pin hides
on a two tier green sloping right to left and back to front
making a birdie here should be worth a punt

Take the driver at **fifteen** to get close to the green
then a pitch and run is the safest shot you'll ever have seen
so long as you don't attack
cos you don't want to go through the back

Par three **sixteenth** is only a nine
but if you're big you'll be fine
so play a soft eight
if bunker shots you hate

A three wood slightly right at hole **seventeen**
then a mid iron from the right to kick down to the green
be careful if you're beyond the pin on a with grain cut
tricky green to hole a downhill putt

Three wood from the **eighteenth** tee
to clear the railway sleepered bunkers you see
guarding the fairway twenty feet above the teeing ground
to trap any low shot for the first hundred yards around
so you need height and accuracy for left centre of fairway
which is the best side to approach the green I'd say
leaving a wedge to the flag
and chance of a birdie to bag

**So there you have a different side
to playing round Irvine Bogside
a course to play cautiously
using your driver sparingly.**

Irvine Ravenspark

If you have a few minutes I'd like
to invite you in due course
to join me for a round of golf
at Ravenspark Golf Course
1907 it opened to bring golf
to the whole community
since then millions have taken
the opportunity

Your **first** tee shot placed down the right opens up the
    green
going left would find deep rough where countless others
    have been
you now have a long pitch between the bunkers to the pin
and a good chance of getting your putt in

Approach the **second** green from the left semi rough
as coming in from the right needs a prayer above
from here it is only an eight or a nine
played between the traps with a fade is the line

Hit your **third** tee shot left to avoid the out of bounds
A sliced shot could cost you more than a few pounds
now a long iron or fairway wood
on the left trap with a fade if you could

Fourth hole par three requires a long iron or wood
to the front left of the green would be good
you now have a fairly long putt to lag
almost the full length of the green to the flag

Hole number **five** needs a well hit drive to the right
then a mid iron to the front half of the green will delight
from where you'll be left with an uphill putt
and every chance of getting your ball in the cup

There's room on the right at hole **six** for a three wood here
leaving the deep rough and gully holding no fear
then a shortish iron could open the door
to marking a birdie as your score

Seventh hole dog legs left and has no room for error
missing the fairway will fill you with terror
Play short of the bunker on the right hand side
then a seven iron to fill you with pride

282 yard par four **eighth** can be reached with one shot
but surrounded by bunkers for your ball to be caught
Lay up with an iron or fairway wood slightly left
then pitch soft and gentle with a touch that is deft
to land on the fringe rolling down to the pin
can leave you a shortish putt to get in
attacking with your pitch won't be much cop
at the back of the green there's a ten foot drop

Dog leg hole number **nine**
should be played every time
with a draw from the tee
then a wedge or a nine

Par five dog leg **tenth** needs a fade at the start
then a three wood not for the faint of heart
the out of bounds eats in close to the green
many have thought about what might have been
but the closer your shot can get to the flag
the easier it will be for your birdie to bag

Then on to the **eleventh** with a score on your mind
and a three wood for safety with a fairway to find
Lay up short of the ridge and with a flat lie
play a seven iron floated in nice and high

Hole **twelve** is long and straight with a fairway that's tight
a long drive then a long iron drawing in from the right
the green throws the ball left towards deep sand
not what you would have originally planned

Thirteenth needs a three wood down the left with a fade
find the fairway from the tee and you're just about made
a mid iron to the green turning in from the right
can kick down to the pin if it's at the right height

Now you're on the last five and the end is in sight
with birdies to be had if you can play them right
you must play with caution and plan your attack
if you want to get some strokes back

Fourteenth tee is an iron or fairway wood
middle right of centre should be good
then a wedge or a nine
coming in on the right hand line

Fifteenth hole par three is surrounded by sand
but a well struck mid iron and another putt could be canned
if not you'll be happy to make a par three
and quickly move on to the next tee

The **sixteenth** is a hole with two bunkers in reach
hit three wood from the tee and the hole is a peach
just a wedge to the green with a birdie as the prize
provided you make the putt the right size

On to the **seventeenth** where the fairway is tight
leave the driver alone the bushes are the wrong height
a fairway wood is wise keeping it nice and straight
avoiding all the gorse that golfers hate
now a short iron to the front half of the green
leaves an uphill putt and no out of bounds seen

Now the **eighteenth** and the end is nigh
but have you the bottle to finish on a high
keep the driver in the bag three wood is best
aim down the right and be up for the test
a second shot short of the left trap is your target
or even creeping on to the edge of the carpet
avoiding the car park to the right of the green
where many have been and have seen
a good score spoiled by a couple of shots
or even worse, by lots
a long putt now from a few yards short
so remember all you've been taught
and avoid a three putt and taking five
that's how to keep your score alive

**Then in to the nineteenth where each stroke you'll
     recall
and while taking refreshment reflect you can't win
     them all.**

Rowallan Castle

*Here at Rowallan Castle between
   the eighteenth green and
   the first tee
they have what they call a money
   hole you see
If your game finishes all square
   after eighteen they have a par three
hole nineteen*

*It's a straight forward mid to short
    iron slightly uphill to the green
and if I may suggest that you play
    it before you start
it may be required to keep you
    and your opponent apart
and if you want your bets to hedge
playing it first could give you an edge*

Drive up the left semi rough at the **first** hole fading right
hit the fairway level or past the bunker and you just might
hit this green with a mid iron
if all your pistons are firing
over the first trap on the left which makes the entrance tight
fading just enough to finish back right

At the **second** hole par three
play a shortish iron from the tee
to the left centre of the target
if you want to stay on the carpet
any shot doing a right turn
will finish in the hidden burn

Inside the right traps with a draw at the **third** hole par five
you might reach this green in two from a big drive
On the right trap with a draw and give it a bit more
if you want a birdie to lower your score

Driver on the left trap with a fade at hole **four**
turning left to right some more
should leave a comfortable mid iron shot
for the right side of the green to be caught

The par three **fifth** hole
is a mid iron hit with your soul
on the right side drawing in
is the right approach to this pin

Over the right trap with a draw at the **sixth** hole par four
a big drive here can open the door
by leaving a mid iron to be seen
fading from the left side of the green

An iron or fairway wood from the tee at the par four
    seventh hole
leaves only a short iron to the flagpole
coming in from the left at height
you have to judge the distance just right

Shortish iron at the par three hole number **eight**
anywhere on the green would be great
but this is a hole you should attack
as there is no trouble at the back

Down the middle with a draw at hole **nine**
anywhere on the left side of the fairway is fine
Hit your second down the right with a fairway wood
then a wedge to the green should be good

From the **tenth** tee par three
a long iron or fairway wood it will need to be
straight at the green with a slight fade
for the back of the green to be made

Driving down the centre fading to the right
to keep a par four at the **eleventh** in sight
the fairway kicks the ball left towards a gully of deep rough
going in there would be just tough
you probably wouldn't even look for your ball
better not to find it but it's your call
if you hit your tee shot in the right place
you'll have made yourself a good case
for a mid iron coming in from the right side
hitting this green could even out a rough ride

The 307 yard **twelfth** hole par four doesn't look hard
but it is a hole which can help or ruin your card
it's called Chris's gamble and is well named
because for this hole to be tamed
requires a drive on the right trap drawing round
hit well and this green in one shot can be found
Overdone can find deep sand on the left side
missing that leaves deep rough for your ball to hide
Best give this drive your best shot
and try and get this green caught

On the left trap with a fade from the **thirteenth** hole par five tee
being uphill to reach the green three shots it will be
but hit your second on the left trap with a fairway wood
now a wedge to the back left of green if you could

Play short of the traps at the par four hole **fourteen**
now a mid iron will set the scene
on the right trap drawing in to the flag
could give a chance of a birdie to bag

Up the right with your drive at the **fifteenth** hole par four
leaves a longish iron to the green or more
drawing in from the right
can reach the back if it's got the height
but not too far there's only twenty yards to avoid spoiling
    your round
should your ball reach the out of bounds
with the bunkers at the front you'll have to wait and see
if it will be a real case of 'Deery Me'

High drive at **sixteen** par five with a draw down the right side
then choose between a fairway wood down the left with a left
    to right slide
Hoping for a good kick and a lot of run
reaching this green would be a lot of fun
or laying up with an iron short of the water on the right
to leave a fuller shot with a wedge over the traps with lots of bite

At the **seventeenth** hole par three
play a long iron from the tee
drawing in from the right hand side
to the left has too many places for your ball to hide

Middle right with your drive at the **eighteenth** hole par four
now a long iron or fairway wood can protect your score
played on the left trap fading right
is the way to finish your fight

**Now if you're all square you can play the money hole
    nineteen
and you've already practised playing to this green
so hopefully you'll hit the shot
that gets the drinks bought.**

Loudoun
Gowf Club

Loudoun Gowf Club was founded
in 1909
and the course has been laid out
just fine

Drive down the middle with a fade to the right
the trees on the left make this **first** hole a bit tight
but a shortish iron played to the left side of the green
will kick down to the pin leaving an uphill putt to be seen

At the **second** play from the tee with a three wood
down the left with a fade should be good
then a short iron to the back
trouble at the front so safe to attack

Three wood again at the **third** hole par four
down the left turning right a bit more
a short iron to the right half
leaves a birdie chance to have

Fourth hole par three
play a mid iron from the tee
fading in from the left hand side
middle back of green can't hide

Fifth hole par five play an iron or fairway wood
short of the burn if you could
then a fairway wood down the middle with a fade
finishing on the right hand side would be well played
giving you a chance with a pitch and putt
to chalk another birdie up

The **sixth** hole dog leg par four
take your three wood once more
down the left fading round
will be sound
leaving a mid to short iron turning in from the right
to finish back left if you might

Down the left with your drive at hole **seven**
just hitting this fairway will be heaven
then a mid to long iron drawing in from the right
hitting this green would be a pretty sight

Play a three wood with a fade at hole **eight**
middle right of fairway will be great
now a mid to short iron on the left trap fading in to the stick
I'd try to leave an uphill putt but take your pick

Lay up with an iron from the tee at hole **nine**
short of the slope will be fine
followed by a shortish iron hit nice and straight
the rest I'm afraid is down to fate

A long iron at the **tenth** hole par three
back of the green is the place to be
two bunkers at the front one left one right
make the entrance to this green tight

Hit a mid iron at **eleven** on the left edge fading in
is the correct approach to this pin
slightly left to the front of the green I'd say
is the safest way in which to play

An iron from the tee at the **twelfth** hole par four
across the burn to the right to protect your score
now a wedge to the left edge drifting right
is the correct way to attack the pin alright
Downwind big hitters can drive the green in one shot
it needs to be inside the burn with a draw to be caught

Inside the left traps fading a three wood at **thirteen**
being short of the right trap sets the scene
for a mid iron drawing over the front trap
to the front fringe avoids the out of bounds at the back

Between the traps with your drive at **fourteen** fading slightly
    right
then a longish iron to a green which at the front is tight
on the left trap with a fade erring slightly strong
middle back of green is where you belong

A three wood down the left with a fade at **fifteen**
leaves a clear approach to this two tier green
a shortish iron on the left edge turning right
is the way to attack this pin with some bite

The par three **sixteenth** hole
needs a fairway wood and a bit of roll
inside the right trap drawing round
is the way to negotiate this piece of ground

At the **seventeenth** hole par three
a mid iron with a fade from the tee
landing back left kicking down to the cup
could leave you the right length of putt

Now the **eighteenth** which is a bit of a test
and will require nothing less than your best
a long drive slightly left with a fade
must hit the fairway for this green to be made
now a long iron or fairway wood
inside the left trap with a fade will be good
if you can two putt for a solid par four
you will indeed have protected your score

**Having played the only Gowf Club in the world
to have its flag unfurled
on this Gowf field
which never had crops to yield
so contemplate while you're having a few beers
they've been playing Gowf here over 400 years!**

Ardeer G.C.

1880 was the year Ardeer Golf Club
*   was founded*
boasting two Open Champions,
*   the members were astounded*
then their Club Champion won two
*   Scottish Amateur titles remember*
so they duly made Hammy McInally
*   a Life Member*

Your **opening** hole is a par three
which will require a long iron from the tee
best played inside the left trap fading in to the right
holding the ball against the slope with some bite

From the **second** tee play your three wood
over the left trap with a fade if you could
beware of the out of bounds all the way down the right
a slice in the wind can get out of hand try as you might
but with only a short iron to play
we won't let the wind get in the way
over the left trap fading in
should get you close enough with some spin

At the **third** with the out of bounds on the right
driving on the left trap with a fade would be bright
being uphill this should leave just a pitch
a birdie should be a snitch

A three wood from the **fourth** tee
up the left side with a fade and see
if you can carry the ridge and stay on the short cut
then it's just a shortish iron to leave you a putt
if hit over the left trap fading round
to the front half rolling down to the pin I've found

The **fifth** hole par five
unless downwind is too long to reach in two off a good drive
so hit a three wood on the left trap fading right
then again down the left side which is tight
now a shortish iron inside the left trap with a fade
should kick down to the pin when all's been said

Drive over the right trap at the **sixth** drawing in for you to pick
a shortish iron to cover the stick
don't be scared to attack
cos the ball will screw back

Over the left trap with your drive
at the **seventh** hole par five
fading in to the centre of the fairway
gives you a chance to reach in two I'd say
a fairway wood on the right trap with some run
and most of your work is done
even if you're short of the front edge
it's an easy chip with a wedge

At the **eighth** hole par three
it's uphill as you can see
a mid iron over the right trap drawing in
is the way to get close to the pin

A three wood from the tee at **nine**
inside the left trap with a fade will be fine
leaves only a wedge to the back
and a chance of a birdie with the right attack

Hit your drive slightly right at the **tenth** hole par four
then a shortish iron remembering to give it a bit more
over the right hand trap drawing in to the flag
to give you the chance of a birdie to bag

Drive up the right at the **eleventh** drawing round
and hopefully the middle of the fairway can be found
you want to hit a mid iron to this green from your tee shot
and perhaps the back of the green can be caught

Up the left with a fade for your drive
at this **twelfth** hole par five
then hit for the left trap with a fairway wood
hoping for a pitch and putt to do you good

From the **thirteenth** tee play a fairway wood
anywhere on the fairway short of the burn if you could
now a longish iron turning in from the right
two bunkers short left make that side tight

Driver or three wood up the hill at **fourteen**
a good hole if one shot can hit this green
with the green and fairway sloping back to front
don't be scared to give it a dunt

Place your drive down the right at the **fifteenth** hole par four
the slope of the fairway will make your ball run a bit more
leaving only a shortish iron on this long hole
to pitch close to the flagpole

You want to hit your drive at **sixteen** fairly straight
anywhere on the fairway will be great
leaving a shortish iron to a two tier green
back right is the place you want to be seen

Down the right again at the **seventeenth** par four
a shortish iron could perhaps open the door
inside the right trap turning in
could finish close with the right amount of backspin

At the **eighteenth** hole par three
play a mid iron from the tee
inside the left trap landing left of the pin
kicking right to finish close enough to get the putt in the tin

There ends your round of golf at Ardeer
don't be concerned if you didn't get near
breaking par or playing to your handicap
because as Arnold would say 'you'll be back!'

West Kilbride

Any flaws in your game
won't be able to hide
as you play golf round
West Kilbride
founded in 1893
right beside the sea

Your **first** tee shot should be a driver or three wood
over the left hand bunker if you could
onto the middle of fairway number eighteen
which gives a nice approach to the first green
leaving your partners full of admiration
for taking the out of bounds out of the equation
you are now only left with a wedge or a nine
back middle of green is fine

Three wood from the **second** tee
down the left with a fade it will be
again you are only left with a wedge or a nine
back right of green is your line

Par five **third**
gives a good chance of bagging a bird
driver inside the left bunker fading round
now a long iron or fairway wood and this green can be found
if you come in from the right hand side
there's nowhere a birdie can hide

Longish iron at the **fourth** hole par three
inside the left trap with a fade it should be
but don't go too far
if you want to make your par

At the **fifth** hole par four
a good drive could open the door
up the left with a fade and see
if a mid iron to the back of the green it will be

Drive up the left at hole number **six**
should leave a shortish stick
to attack the green
for another par to be seen

Seventh hole par five
needs a left hand side drive
inside the left bunker with a fade
unless downwind this green can't be made
so play your second between the two traps on the right
now with only a wedge you just might
hit it close enough to make a four
and help improve your score

Hit driver off the tee at **eight**
inside the left traps with a fade will be great
leaving a solid mid iron to the back right
where you can make a par four without much of a fight

A longish iron at the **ninth** hole par three
inside the left trap with a fade is key
to finishing front right
as to the back is tight

Driver from the tee at **ten**
inside the out of bounds fence with a fade then
a mid iron over the left hand trap with a fade
and a good par four can be made

The **eleventh** par four hole
depending on the wind, your score and the flagpole
take a driver or three wood
on the right trap with a draw would be good
leaving a good chance of a three
then on to the next tee

Twelfth hole par three
is surrounded by sand you see
and requires a perfect mid to long iron strike
over the bunkers on the right if you like

Thirteenth's a driver inside the left trap fading in
now a mid to longish iron straight at the pin
long green so make sure you are up
you'll be happy with two putts to get your ball in the cup

316 yard **fourteenth** hole par four you might like
it could improve your score if you get on your bike
hit your drive on the right trap with a draw and hope
that you are left with some scope
to get down in two more
to lower your score

Fifteen's a driver on the left trap from the tee
then a strong mid iron to the back left it will be
because have no fear
it will take two good putts from the bottom tier

Drive on the left trap at **sixteen**
leaving only a wedge to the green
landing on the front to run down to the cup
is your best chance of a pitch and a putt

Aim your drive at the **seventeenth** up the right
with a right to left flight
finishing on the left side
when the fairway takes it for a ride
now a mid iron to the right of the flag
then another par is in the bag

Eighteen's a driver inside the bunker on the right
now a short iron just might
produce a nice figure to be had
looking good on your score card

**After that round you may feel washed up with the tide
but that's the beauty of playing West Kilbride.**

Largs Kelburn

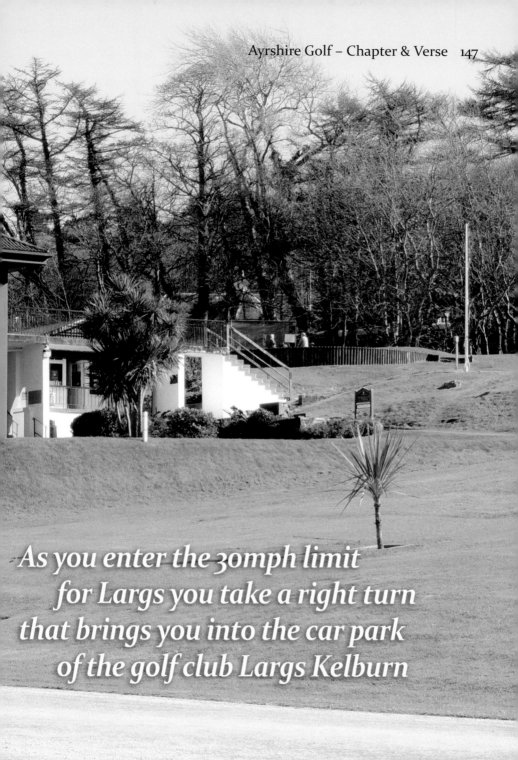

*As you enter the 30mph limit
    for Largs you take a right turn
that brings you into the car park
    of the golf club Largs Kelburn*

This **first** hole par three
is only a seven or eight iron from the tee
but it's uphill all the way
and if you are short you will pay
the ball will roll back fifty yards
so it's vital on the tee you play all your cards
and fully commit to your tee shot
as it's important this green is caught
once there it's almost certain you'll have an uphill putt
so make sure your first putt is up

At the **second** hole par four drive down the left with a fade
it is then a mid iron for the green to be made
err middle front of the green to avoid trouble at the back
it is not a green you want to attack

Drive inside the right trap with a draw at the **third** hole par five
this green can be reached in two if you hit a good drive
with a long iron or fairway wood
on the right trap with a draw if you could

Par three hole number **four**
is a longish iron from the tee to its core
on the left trap fading round
is the way for this green to be found
erring slightly left and long
back left is where you belong

Launch your drive at the left trap with a fade at hole **five**
reaching this green with a good drive can keep your hopes alive
if not a good pitch
can bag a birdie if it goes without a hitch

From the **sixth** tee play your three wood
down the right with a draw would be good
then a shortish iron to the back right
two bunkers at the front make the entrance tight

Inside the left trap with a fade for your drive at the **seventh** hole
    par four
leaves a mid iron on the left trap with a fade to help your score
with a bunker short left and three on the right hand side
err long and left as anything to the right gets a rough ride

At the par three hole number **eight**
a mid iron drawing in from the right would be great
landing on the carpet and running up
somewhere close enough to the cup

Play a fairway wood from the tee at **nine**
inside the trees on the right should be fine
then a mid to shortish iron played with a fade
will need to make the top tier when all's been said

A three wood again from the **tenth** tee
down the right with a draw is the place to be
then a mid iron turning left to right
should hold this green if it's got some bite

Eleventh tee is a long iron or fairway wood
slightly right of the marker if you could
then a mid to short iron to a plateau green
and a tricky par can be seen

On the right trap with a draw for your drive at the par five hole
  twelve
then into your bag for a big stick you must delve
A three wood drawing in from the right trap
can make the putting surface if there's no mishap

Three wood from the **thirteenth** tee
middle right of fairway is the place to be
mid to short iron to the middle left of pin
can give you a chance of a win

The **fourteenth** hole par three
back of green is where you want to be
mid to short iron inside the right trap drawing round
should achieve this I'll be bound

Down the right with a draw at **fifteen**
then a fairway wood to the green
on the right hand trap drawing in
trying not to go beyond the pin

An iron from the tee at **sixteenth** hole
still leaves a short iron to the flagpole
not worth the risk to carry the burn
there's too much trouble at every turn

Play from the tee at **seventeen** with a fairway wood
then it's only a wedge to the green if you could
played with feel and precision
will cement your decision

Eighteen's a three wood from the tee
leaves only a shortish iron to the green you see
played to the right of the pin is your plan of attack
to get your putt in you need to be at the back

**Providing you can stay out of the burn
you'll enjoy Largs Kelburn.**

Largs Routenburn

Be sure to choose a nice day
to have some fun
and enjoy the views playing golf
at Largs Routenburn
the course where a young
Sam Torrance learned his game
before his tournament successes
and Ryder Cup fame

A tough **opening** hole here
one to respect and fear
a long iron fading in from the left edge
keeping well away from the out of bounds hedge

Drive down the middle at the **second** hole par four
the ground will take the ball to the left a little more
now a mid iron to the right allowing for the slope of the ground
is the best way for this green to be found

Three wood at the **third** down the left for a fuller second shot
it's vital for your score that this green is caught
a wedge hit to the right of the pin
trying not to put on too much backspin

Up the left for your drive at the **fourth** with a fade
a good fairway wood and this green can be made
played down the left side holding its line
if you don't reach a pitch and putt will do fine

At the **fifth** hole par three
a comfortable mid iron it will be
played slightly left of the pin
then hope you can get your putt in

Hit your drive up the middle at hole **six**
then you can choose one of your shorter sticks
to attack the flag on a narrow green
holing the putt remains to be seen

Play a fairway wood from the **seventh** tee
leaving you a full shot you see
to attack with some backspin
to leave your ball below the pin

Par three hole number **eight**
anywhere on the green will be great
a shortish club it will be
no more than an eight or a nine from the tee

Good drive required at hole **nine**
down the middle with a fade is fine
shortish iron slightly left of the pin
should give you a chance to get a putt in

Hole number **ten** drive straight and long
leaving a pitch to where you belong
landing slightly left and rolling round
to where a birdie could be found

Left sided drive at **eleven** nice and high
it will bounce to the right when it falls from the sky
leaving a pitch aimed slightly left
played with a touch that is deft

This **twelfth** hole par five
depends so much on your drive
if you finish on the fairway from the tee
you will be amazed that you can be
only a mid iron away from the green
land it short to run on old bean

Thirteenth needs a mid to long iron at this par three
down the left side with a fade it shall be
keep well away from the out of bounds on the right
going in there would not be a pretty sight

From the **fourteenth** tee drive down the right side of the fairway
you can get close to this green I'd say
you'll be left with just a pitch and run
landing short right will yield a birdie for some

A mid iron at the par three hole **fifteen**
landing short left to run on to the green
remembering all the greens run to the sea
can give you the edge for making a birdie

An iron or fairway wood from the tee at **sixteen**
avoids the out of bounds where many others have been
pitch slightly left as it will break to the right
tricky to get close try as you might

Big drive down the left at the **seventeenth** par five
the ball will kick to the right for the best line from a good drive
now a long iron or wood aimed at the left trap should suffice
so long as it slides to the right and is hit nice

Mid to shortish iron from the tee
at this **eighteenth** hole par three
don't overclub and hit it long
better to underclub than to be strong.

Well did you see any submarines sailing up the Clyde?
from the top of the course even submerged they cannot
   hide.

Golf Club Specifics

Club Name: ARDEER
Date Founded: 1880 (originally a 9 hole course, relocated in 1905, 18 hole course relocated again in 1965)
Course Architect: Strutt – 1965
Tournaments Hosted: None
Tournament Winners: N/A
Famous Members:
- Hamilton McInally (Scottish Amateur Champion 1937, 1939 & 1947).
- Jackie Cannon (Scottish Amateur Championship 1969).
- Jamie Anderson (British Open Championship 1877, 1878 & 1879).
- Willie Fernie (British Open Championship 1883)

Club Name: AYR BELLEISLE
Date Founded: 1927
Course Architect: James Braid
Tournaments Hosted:
British Ladies Strokeplay 1971
Scottish Coca Cola Tournament
Turnberry European Open Qualifying 1978
Sunderland Masters 1998
Tournament Winners: N/A

Club Name: BALLOCHMYLE
Date Founded: 1937
Course Architect: N/A
Tournaments Hosted: None
Tournament Winners: N/A
Historic Moment: Robert Burns wrote 'The Bonnie Lass o' Ballochmyle' while walking through the estate in 1786.
Signature Hole: ELEVENTH ('Clootie's Corner' 413 yards, par-4) – A 90-degree dogleg right. To reach the dogleg requires a carry of 180 yards between trees on both sides and over a burn running across the fairway.

Club Name: BRUNSTON CASTLE
Date Founded: Mid 1990s
Course Architect: Donal Steel
Tournaments Hosted: None
Tournament Winners: N/A

Club Name: DUNDONALD LINKS
Date Founded: 2003
Course Architect: Kyle Phillips
Tournaments Hosted:
   Ladies Scottish Open 2015
Tournament Winners: Rebecca Artis

Club Name: GLASGOW GAILES
Date Founded: 1892
Course Architect: Willie Park Jnr
Tournaments Hosted:
- Open Championship sole Scottish venue Final Qualifying 2014 to 2017
- Open Championship Final Qualifying to Troon or Turnberry Opens since 1973
- British Youths Open Amateur Championship
- British Seniors Open Amateur Championship
- Scottish Seniors Open Amateur Strokeplay Championship
- Scottish Open Amateur Strokeplay
- Scottish Amateur Championship
- Scottish PGA Championship
- Scottish Golf Union Home Internationals 2012
- R&A Amateur Championship Qualifying 2102
- Palmer Cup 2008 Europe v USA College/University golf match
Tournament Winners: N/A

Club Name: IRVINE BOGSIDE

When the club hosted an early pro tournament in 1904 among those attending were golf legends Old Tom Morris and James Braid, who went on to redesign the course in 1926.

Three Scottish Amateur Champions – Hamilton McInally, Jack Cannon and James Walker who honed their skills at the course – grew up a stone's throw away, in the former mining village of Bartonholm – the 15th hole is now named after it.

Date Founded: 1887

Course Architect: James Braid

Tournaments Hosted:
- Open Championship Final Qualifying to Troon or Turnberry Opens
- British Amateur Championships
- British Ladies Final 2001

Tournament Winners: N/A

Club Name: IRVINE RAVENSPARK

European Tour and Tartan Tour Professional, and author of this book Peter Bond, learned to play golf here.

He returned in 1982 until present day as Club Professional, and represented the club on both tours until retiring from competitive golf in 1994.

Date Founded: 1907

Course Architect: Mr Tulloch of Gailes

Tournaments Hosted: Co-hosted the Scottish Amateur Stroke Play twice with Irvine Bogside G.C. in the 1980s.

Tournament Winners: N/A

Club Name: KILMARNOCK BARASSIE

Date Founded: 1887

Course Architect: N/A

Tournaments Hosted:
- Final Qualifying for 2012 Senior Open Championship
- Scottish Amateur Strokeplay Championship 2012
- Boys Amateur Championship 2010
- Final Qualifying for the Open Championship 2009

- Scottish Ladies Amateur Championship 2007
- Junior Open (R&A) 2004
- Final Qualifying for Senior Open Championship 2003
- Ladies Amateur Championship 2001
- Final Qualifying for Amateur Championship 2001
- European Youth Championship 2000

Club Name: LARGS KELBURNE

Date Founded: 1891

Course Architect: Willie Campbell

Tournaments Hosted: None

Tournament Winners: N/A

Club Name: LARGS ROUTENBURN

Date Founded: 1914

Course Architect: James Braid

Tournaments Hosted: None

Tournament Winners: N/A

Famous Members: European Tour and Ryder Cup legend Sam Torrance honed his craft here, under the tuition of his father Bob Torrance, himself a leading golf tutor and mentor to many of today's leading golfers.

Club Name: LOUDOUN

Date Founded: 1908

Course Architect: Mr Hydes, who after laying out the original 18 holes was paid an honorarium of £1.05.

Tournaments Hosted: None

Tournament Winners: N/A

The only Gowf Club in the world.

Was the private gowf field of the Loudoun family for over 400 years, and the ground has never been ploughed.

Club Name: OLD PRESTWICK

Date Founded: 1851

Course Architect: Tom Morris

Tournaments Hosted:
- Open Championship 1860 – 1870, 1872,

1875, 1878, 1881, 1884, 1887, 1890, 1893, 1898, 1903, 1908, 1914 & 1925
- British Ladies' Open Amateur Strokeplay Championship 2013
- 100th Scottish Ladies Amateur Championship 2014
- Hosted eleven Amateur Championships between 1888 and 2001
- Scottish Amateur Championships

Club Name: PRESTWICK ST. NICHOLAS
Date Founded: 1851
Course Architect: Tom Morris
Tournaments Hosted:
- Open Qualifying 1986
Tournament Winners: N/A
Old Tom Morris was a founder member.

Club Name: PRESTWICK ST. CUTHBERT
Date Founded: 1851
Course Architect: Tom Morris
Tournaments Hosted: St. Cuthbert have not held any major events such as the Scottish Amateur etc, however in 1999, the club centenary year, they hosted their first Scottish national event, the Scottish Boys Area Team Championship, which was held again at the club in 2013, the 50th anniversary of the opening of the present course.
The club has also hosted the Ayrshire Boys, Ayrshire Mens and Ayrshire Ladies Championships on a number of occasions, and continues to be a regular venue for county matches.

Club Name: ROWALLAN CASTLE
Date Founded: 2010
Course Architect: Colin Montgomerie
Tournaments Hosted: None
Tournament Winners: N/A

Club Name: ROYAL TROON
In 2016 Royal Troon hosts its NINTH Open Championship. The course is where former Ryder Cup Captain and record

winner of the European Tour Order of Merit Colin Montgomerie learned to play. The club was awarded Royal status in 1978 to commemorate its centenary.
Date Founded: 1878
Course Architect: Charlie Hunter
Tournaments Hosted:
- Open Championship 1923, 1950, 1962, 1973, 1982, 1989, 1997, 2004 & 2016
- Senior British Open
- Amateur Championship
Tournament Winners: N/A

Club Name: SEAFIELD
Date Founded: 1976
Course Architect: N/A
Tournaments Hosted: None
Tournament Winners: N/A

Club Name: TROON DARLEY
Date Founded: 1910
Course Architect: N/A
Tournaments Hosted: None
Tournament Winners: N/A

Club Name: TROON LOCHGREEN
Was the Open Championship qualifying course in 1962 when Jack Nicklaus qualified for his first Open, held at Royal Troon and won by Arnold Palmer.

Club Name: TRUMP KINTYRE
Date Founded: 2001
Course Architect: Donald Steel
Tournaments Hosted:
- Open Championship Final Qualifying 2004
Signature Hole: Kintyre's Cove (8th Hole) involves a drive from an elevated tee towards the sea and an unforgettable blind second shot to the green set in a gully by the rocks. Unseen from the tee, hidden by a narrow ridge, the green is in a cove that seems to merge with the craggy beach beyond.

Club Name:
TRUMP TURNBERRY AILSA
Named after the Marquess of Ailsa.
Date Founded: 1902
Course Architect: William Fernie
Tournaments Hosted:
- Open Championship 1977, 1986, 1994, 2004
- Senior Open Championship 1987, 1988, 1989, 1990, 2003, 2006, 2012
- Womens British Open 2002 & 2015

Tournament Winners: N/A

Club Name: WESTERN GAILES
Date Founded: 1897
Course Architect: Tom Morris
Tournaments Hosted:
- 1903 – Open Professional Tournament promoted by Western Gailes won by Harry Vardon
- 1923 – Scottish Professional Championship won by A.W. Butchart (Barassie)
- 1927 – Scottish Amateur Championship won by Andrew Jamieson
- 1934 – Scottish Amateur Championship won by Jack McLean for the third successive time
- 1946 – International match Scotland versus England. England won 10 – 8
- 1953 – Scottish Amateur Championship won by D.A. Blair
- 1961 – Scottish Amateur Championship won by J. Walker
- 1964 – PGA Championship won by Tony Grubb – of note, after 36 holes a Western Gailes member (Billy Jack) led the tournament
- 1966 – Scottish Amateur Championship won by R.D.B.M. Shade – his third of five consecutive victories
- 1972 – Curtis Cup won by USA 10 – 8
- 1974 – Scottish Amateur Championship won by G.H. Murray
- 1981 – Scottish Amateur Championship won by C. R. Dalgleish who went on to play and manage GB & NI in the Walker Cup
- 1984 – British Seniors Amateur Championship won by John Owens (USA)
- 1989 – Jack Gow – a Western Gailes member – played the 13th and 15th holes each in one shot in the same round. He used the same ball and club at each hole.
- 1996 – Scottish Seniors Open Championship won by Charlie Green (Dumbarton)
- 1998 – British Seniors Amateur Championship won by David Lane (England)
- 2002 – Scottish Amateur Championship won by A. McArthur (Scotland)
- 2007 – European Men's Amateur Team Championship (notable players include Rory McIlroy, Shane Lowry, Ritchie Ramsay): Gold Medal – Ireland (beat France 41/2-21/2); Silver Medal – France; Bronze – Scotland (beat England 4-3)
- 2011 - Scottish Amateur Championship won by D. Law (Scotland)

Club Name: WEST KILBRIDE
Date Founded: 1893
Course Architect: Tom Morris, redesigned by James Braid in 1905
Tournaments Hosted:
- Scottish Boys' Championship